The Awakened Psychic

About the Author

Kala Ambrose is your travel guide to the other side. She is the award-winning author of five books including *The Awakened Aura*, a national columnist, an inspirational speaker and teacher, and host of the *Explore Your Spirit with Kala Show*. Kala Ambrose's teachings are described as enlightening, empowering, and inspiring. Visit her online at ExploreYourSpirit.com

WHAT YOU NEED TO KNOW TO DEVELOP
YOUR PSYCHIC ABILITIES

The Awakened Psychic

Kala Ambrose

Llewellyn Publications
Woodbury, Minnesota

FIRST EDITION
First Printing, 2016

Cover image: iStockphoto.com/24613434/©Naddiya;
iStockphoto.com/80695773/©stereohype
Cover design: Ellen Lawson

Llewellyn Publications is a registered trademark of Llewellyn Worldwide Ltd.

Library of Congress Cataloging-in-Publication Data
Names: Ambrose, Kala, author.
Title: The awakened psychic : what you need to know to develop your psychic
abilities / by Kala Ambrose.
Description: First edition. | Woodbury, MN : Llewellyn Publications, a
Division of Llewellyn Worldwide Ltd., [2016] | Includes bibliographical
references.
Identifiers: LCCN 2016023385 (print) | LCCN 2016034203 (ebook) | ISBN
9780738749013 | ISBN 9780738750262 ()
Subjects: LCSH: Psychic ability. | Psychics.
Classification: LCC BF1031 .A465 2016 (print) | LCC BF1031 (ebook) |
DDC
133.8—dc23
LC record available at https://lccn.loc.gov/2016023385

Llewellyn Publications
A Division of Llewellyn Worldwide Ltd.
2143 Wooddale Drive
Woodbury, MN 55125.2989
www.llewellyn.com

Printed in the United States of America

Other Books by Kala Ambrose

Dedication

This book is dedicated to Tim Ambrose—
my champion, my best friend, and my loving guide in this
lifetime and many others.

Contents

Introduction

I don't remember when I first heard the term "psychic." In my world, the concept had always been referred to by different names. I grew up in Louisiana, where people who had this ability were referred to as those who had "the sight," had "the gift," "knew" things, or "walked with spirit."

My parents realized early on that I had psychic ability. It wasn't a surprise to them, as others in my family, including my grandfather and my great-grandmother, had similar gifts. My great-grandmother supported her family reading tea leaves and tarot cards, and my mother also had psychic abilities. Over time I've seen that almost everyone in my family is intuitive in one form or another.

Many times I've referred to myself as a reluctant medium. Since childhood I have been able to see spirits, and they love to interact with me. The first time I saw my great-grandmother in spirit, she appeared in my bedroom and chatted with me one evening after my grandfather had died. I don't remember my exact age, but I would say I was around eleven or twelve years old. She appeared one evening while I was in bed reading and sat on the edge of my bed. Looking up over my book,

I took her in—her dress, shoes, hair, and unique sense of style. As my eyes met hers, she hopped up from the bed and began to pace back and forth in my room.

"I don't know if I should be here," she said. "Your grandfather is against me visiting you."

"Why would Papa not want you to visit me?" I inquired.

My grandfather had recently passed away, and he was a very intuitive person who used his abilities to help people in his own way.

The night he died I woke from my dreams, sensing he was in mortal danger and was about to die. I could feel his stress and loved him so much.

At that very stressful moment in my childhood, I asked God and the angels to spare his life and to take my life instead in trade. In what I conceived to be a spiritual and sacrificial request, I prepared for God to come take my life so that my grandfather would live. I waited and waited. After a few minutes of nothing happening, I took a deep breath and could feel my grandfather's energy diminishing as his life force grew weaker.

I began to cough, choking on what felt like phlegm in my lungs. As I struggled to clear my throat, I realized I was feeling what my grandfather was going through. I didn't know the terminology that explained that I was an empath, but I was already very familiar with feeling other people's suffering, both physically and emotionally.

I jumped off my bed and ran into my parents' bedroom, waking them both. I was screaming, "Save him—save Papa! He's dying!" My parents both sat up, and my mother pulled me onto the bed.

She said, "Honey, you must have overheard our conversation earlier. We didn't tell you; Papa is in the hospital, but it's nothing to worry about. He had a very minor surgery and is fully recovered. We are going in the morning to bring him home from the hospital."

"No," I cried. "He's not okay. He's choking—he's dying. I asked God to take my life instead, but he won't take my life. I begged him and the angels to take me, but they won't take me. He's dying. Help him."

I began to cry hysterically, and as my mother attempted to comfort me, the phone rang. My father picked up the phone, and after a moment, he looked over at my mother. He was very calm during the conversation, even after he hung up the phone.

He told my mother that he would be right back. Taking my hand, he brought me back to my bed, tucked me in, and told me that he would take care of everything. He asked me to get some sleep and said he would come get me in the morning.

The next sound I remember hearing is my mother sobbing from her room. My father had given her the news he received from that phone call. My beloved grandfather passed away, just as I said. He died suddenly and unexpectedly from an undetected blood clot that burst and filled his lungs with blood. He choked to death on the blood, which I had experienced empathically with my own choking.

I remember the funeral and my mother's gray, ashen face and aura as she dealt with the shock of this loss. I remember my grandmother's pain as she cried for weeks without stopping, not even able to get out of her bed. And I remember my anger, my anger with God for not sparing his life and taking mine. Up until that time, I had been a very religious and devout young Catholic girl. I did not speak to God again for many years. We've since made up, but nothing will ever take away the pain of losing my grandfather. Then came that evening when my great-grandmother, my grandfather's mother, appeared in my room. She was acting suspiciously like she would get in big trouble if she were caught here by someone, though she never said who that someone was.

"Who are you?" I asked her. She stopped to look at me, her hand lightly stroking my face.

"I'm your *grand-mère*," she replied and then began to speak to me in French, of which I knew very little. Growing up in Louisiana, I picked up a few phrases and words but not enough to have an entire conversation in the French language.

She wanted to tell me her story, but I cut her off with all the patience of a young girl, asking if she'd seen my grandfather and if I could please see him.

"I'm afraid not. He's not available at this time." I was heartbroken by this news. She pressed on, as if realizing her time was short. She began to get to the point of her visit, which was to tell me I have the same abilities as my grandfather.

"I know," I said. "Papa and I talked about this several times."

"Yes," she said, "but what he didn't tell you is that you have more abilities than you know about, and some of those come from me. I'm here to give these to you now." She reached forward and gave me one strong tap on my forehead with her finger in what is described as the third-eye area. It felt like a snap, like when you bite into a tough cookie and break it in half. It was like she opened up something deep inside of me that was now set free.

I fell into a deep sleep at that point. I never saw my great-grandmother again in spirit form, though she came into my dreams several other times to either warn me about something or to deliver a message. It was always brief, to the point, and in French.

Later as I explored how to do psychic and medium work, I never worried how I would read for people who spoke a foreign language. When they speak from the spirit world, I hear the language. As spirits speak, pictures that tell the story form around them, so there isn't a big language barrier. The communication is telepathic in nature.

At this point, though, I had been seeing spirits since I was young but had assumed most of them were guardian angels and loving, caring spirits. Now that my connection to the other side had progressed from seeing higher beings of light to seeing the spirits of family members in the form of their most recent lifetime, I wasn't sure if I wanted to continue being a medium. Because I am an empath, seeing them made me incredibly sad. I missed these people and wanted them back here with me or wanted to go where they were. Both options were impossible, so I found it lonely and frustrating.

However, once the veil is pierced in any type of psychic or medium work, the door never stays fully shut again. On the other side, word got out that this young, redheaded girl could communicate with spirit, and I began to get a lot of nightly visitors. They would crowd around, sometimes wanting me to give a message to someone and at other times just wanting me to listen to their stories.

I didn't have the skill set yet to know how to send them away or to understand when enough was enough, so they would drain my energy throughout the night. Many mornings I would wake up with a headache and stomachache, not knowing how to explain this to my mother. She thought that I was just trying to get out of going to school, but I enjoyed school and the break it brought from dealing with the spirits in the evening.

Through my teen years and early twenties, I pushed away my mediumship as much as I could. Most of the time when someone visited in spirit form, it was due to a tragedy. The person had died and wanted to get a message or warning to someone. Many of the souls who tried to speak with me were in a state of despair and confusion. I didn't feel comfortable or qualified at that time to try to find their families and explain that I had a message for them from their dead loved one. It was sad and overwhelming: I just wanted to be a normal teenage girl.

Today, mediumship is a more accepted practice, and people are open to these types of communications. Back when I was growing up, however, talk like that could end up getting you exorcised—or worse, locked up in a mental institution. I had dreams and past-life memories of being burned at the stake, tortured, locked up, and killed for sharing my psychic and medium gifts. It took me many years to overcome these fears in order to be who I was meant to be in this lifetime.

On the other hand, I was enjoying my growing psychic abilities because they dealt with the living, in the here and now. I was training in the magical arts by this time, learning how to do astrology charts and read the tarot, and I was very interested in learning how to develop my psychic abilities and enhance my dream interpretation work. These were all skills that allowed me to help the living and make a difference in their lives. I've come a long way in this lifetime in order to embrace my psychic and mediumship abilities. Both of my books about the haunted history of North Carolina and New Orleans show my ability to connect with both earthbound ghosts and otherworldly spirits in order to gather their stories and share them with the world.

From training for years as a psychic medium, I've learned how to create boundaries and to set the pace and tone for when I'm available to speak with the other side and for how long. I've also learned how to set the intention for spirits to come through from a higher plane of existence only and how to banish the lower-level astral plane spirits. I also now interact with ghosts and understand the different types and how best to communicate with them.

Some mediums work through a "medium guide" on the other side. Typically this is one of their spirit guides who protects them, filters the information from the other side, and delivers it directly to the medium, providing them with the information to relay in readings. This is not the way it works for me. My spirit guides are present and around, but when I ask them for their assistance, they smile, politely shake their head, and say, "It's your journey now to do this without our assistance. You are meant to go directly to the source and be a conduit."

What has happened over the years as I learned to be a "direct conduit" could fill another book. I have interacted with powerful beings of light, faced encounters with beings from the dark side, and seen ghosts from every walk of life. I am forever changed by these experiences and have a very healthy respect for all that goes on in the various planes on the other side. I can only shake my head when someone tells me that there is nothing bad on the other side, for I have seen and experienced the difference. To say that it does not exist makes no logical sense. We come from a place of duality, of light and dark, hot and cold, summer and winter.

It makes sense that if there are higher levels of light beings, there are also lower levels of shadow beings. If you've seen beings of light, you know that it's a wonderful sight to behold. If you haven't seen beings of dark, be thankful.

During your exploration of these abilities, you may find that you have both intuitive or psychic ability and mediumship ability. If you have mediumship ability, you'll want to train with someone who can help you work through the layers of the veil on the other side so that you understand what types of spirits, entities, and beings that you are meeting.

I'm doing my best to touch on so many aspects of the psychic world in this book that I can't truly cover all of the aspects of mediumship ability here. Not everyone has mediumship ability, and many people are not comfortable doing this type of work communicating with the dead. Yet almost everyone I work with is interested in having psychic ability in order to see the future or understand people and situations on a deeper level.

In fact, by working with students from all over the world for the past eighteen years, I've found that everyone I meet has some form of psychic or intuitive ability. The only difference is the strength of their natural ability and how open they are to working with their gifts.

Psychic abilities are like all other natural talents. We have some inherent talent that can get us started, and then it's up to us to work on and hone the ability to turn it into something greater.

As a psychic consultant and teacher, I enjoy helping people understand what is happening in their life from a spiritual perspective so that they can find solutions to their problems and live a better life. Sometimes we need someone who can help shed light on what is going on in our lives. In my consultations, I can see clearly and provide this information to my clients, whose thoughts and emotions are clouded by the problems they are facing.

For more than twenty-five years, I've offered my psychic services in almost every type of situation possible to clients around the world, from the basic consultations with questions regarding love, relationships, families, and children, to questions regarding health and wealth. My clients range from ages twenty to eighty and have a wide variety of spiritual and cultural beliefs. I've read for twenty-somethings who are just starting out in the world, wanting to make their way and their mark, to powerful VPs and CEOs running businesses. As a person with psychic ability, I consult with clients who have a wide variety of interests and passions. Some of them come to me for my work called "entrepreneur intuition." I have the ability to see future trends regarding fashion, real estate, home decor, careers, and technology, to name a few. I offer this helpful information to clients who are building a business or wanting to expand their career. Seeing what trends will be the most popular in the future helps my clients decide what business they should build or create, along with the time frame of when this type of business will lose popularity. This allows them to maximize their profit potential for their business or career and also provides them with the knowledge of the best time to sell their business and start something new or change careers. I also have the ability to assist clients in building their brand, showing them how to connect their intuitive, creative side with their thought-oriented, logical side in order to see how their passion can be translated into a viable business or career.

Other clients come to me for my psychic work in seeing the aura and the akashic records. When consulting with my clients, I see the layers of the aura: the physical, mental, emotional, and spiritual layers. As I scan these layers, I can see what is going on in their lives, including how their thoughts and emotions are affecting the outcome of their goals and desires. I also see karmic markers in the aura, which have been placed there from previous lifetimes and from their actions in this lifetime. I have the ability to travel back and forth to the akashic records on the spiritual planes and obtain information from these soul records. I can then help my clients understand why certain situations, directly related to previous lifetimes and karma, are appearing in their lives. This information is life altering when clients understand why a certain person or situation keeps repeating in their lives. Once they understand why it is occurring, they can change their actions and reactions to the situation, which allows them to fully understand and resolve the encounter. When this occurs, the karmic markers in the aura energy field dissolve, and this particular situation does not come up again.

Some clients like to book ongoing consultations with me in order to maximize the potential of this helpful information regarding their career, business, or relationships. In this capacity, I become their psychic counsultant and help them build a vision plan for long-term goals so that they can turn their dreams into reality. There are also times, though, when we need to trust our gut instincts and listen to the clear, still voice speaking to us from within. For clients who are ready to delve deeper, I move from being their psychic consultant, providing information to them from the other side, to their psychic coach, teaching them how to become psychic themselves so that they can read for themselves and for others.

I teach psychic ability to people who have discovered they are intuitive and want to learn how to work with these abilities and use them in their daily lives. As a wisdom teacher, I've helped a wide variety of people with different skill sets learn how to tap into their intuition and their psychic abilities.

Some of my students develop their psychic abilities in order to have stronger relationships with the people in their lives, while many others want to connect with spirit on a deeper level in order to expand their relationship with their higher self and communicate with their spirit guides, with the aim to live their highest and best life experience.

The work that I do is immensely fulfilling. Every day I help people tap into their psychic abilities and discover who they are at a spiritual level.

It is my belief that at this time we are in the midst of an evolution in which the veil is lifting between the earth plane and the spiritual planes. People around the world are awakening to their sixth sense, which has actually been with them the entire time, and harnessing it. It no longer has to be a mystery. Everyone has intuitive ability at some level.

In this book, we'll explore the various types of psychic ability so you can determine if you have them and, if so, what type or types.

We'll look at how to open up your psychic abilities and how they can be a helpful tool in making decisions regarding following your dreams, enhancing your relationships, and building a business or career that you enjoy. Harnessing these powers is not as difficult as you may believe.

I want to show you how to tap into your own psychic ability so that you can manifest your destiny to the best of your talent, skills, and natural-born abilities.

You have the wisdom within you, waiting to be awakened. As your travel guide to the other side, I'll walk you through each step to tuning in to your psychic abilities.

Let the journey begin.

One

DISCOVER YOUR
HIDDEN PSYCHIC TALENTS

Three items are required for engaging with your psychic self—an open heart, an open mind, and the desire to become a conduit between this world and the other side. You may have already experienced flashes of psychic abilities without even knowing what they were.

Answer these questions to determine signs of awakening to your intuitive abilities:

- Do you sense the energy vibe in a room when you walk into it?
- Do friends turn to you for advice because you get right to the root of their problem?
- Do you often have a gut feeling about a person, such as being untrustworthy, only to ignore that feeling and be proven right later on?
- Have you had a dream that came true for yourself or others? What about dreams about past lives?

- Have you asked for help and noticed synchronicities or signs that appeared to send you a message?
- Do you feel a stirring deep inside of you, an unexplainable longing that says there's more to your life than what you are currently experiencing?
- Have you felt the presence of a loved one in spirit around you and seen signs that they are near?
- Do you find yourself thinking about someone out of the blue, and then the phone rings as this person calls you?
- Do you feel deeply connected to nature and the elements? Do storms excite you?

If you've experienced any of these phenomena, you are awakening to your intuitive abilities.

When you are open to your natural intuitive abilities, you have the potential to escape the confines of time and space in order to see beyond the veil of this world into the spirit realms. With this ability, you are able to see the future and the past, to connect with spirits and loved ones on the other side, and to explore what is described as the greater mysteries.

What does "being psychic" mean? Let's begin by defining the types of psychic abilities.

Clairvoyance

The term "clairvoyance" comes from the French language. *Clair* means "clear" and *voyance* means "sight" or a psychic vision, so to be clairvoyant is to have "clear (psychic) sight." Wouldn't it be fun to go to the eye doctor for a test, and upon finding your vision to be 20/20, he would declare you clairvoyant? But alas, there is no clear test at this time for sixth-sense divination.

Clairvoyance, like all of the clair abilities, is a form of extrasensory perception (ESP). People who have clairvoyant abilities are also described in modern times as psychics and intuitives with the gift of precognition. Basically it means to have the ability to see future events before they occur in what we call "real time" or third-dimensional earth time. Basically, it is to see beyond time and space.

It also means seeing people, places, things, events, and the aura around a person that have not been disclosed to the psychic reader. With this ability, some clairvoyants help solve mysteries, crimes, and missing person cases and help locate lost objects.

Clairvoyants have served as guides to kings, queens, and other royalty throughout the history of the world. They've also been referred to as oracles and sibyls.

Many clairvoyants first discover that they have psychic ability by having dreams that come true. This causes them to look into the possibility of intuition and prophecy. Once they begin to explore this thought, it opens their minds to the possibilities. Memories of having visions and communicating with spirit in childhood, before they pushed the ability away or were told that it wasn't real, begin to resurface.

As clairvoyants learn to interpret their dreams, they find that their psychic visions also begin to occur when they are awake. The two practices, dream interpretations and psychic visions, work hand in hand, each helping those with psychic ability further develop their understanding of what they are seeing intuitively on the conscious and subconscious levels.

Many clairvoyants move on from dream interpretations and experiencing psychic visions to also being able to travel through the spiritual planes to visit the akashic records through astral travel. The akashic records, which are also described as the Hall of Records, are where the records of each soul are recorded and stored from lifetime to lifetime in the spirit world. The actions of each person are placed in these books of records throughout each lifetime. Each time a person passes on from a lifetime, they return to the akashic records to review their lifetime from the perspective of their higher self. When the soul returns to the earth plane for another lifetime, any unfinished business from a previous lifetime is imprinted in the aura energy field of their soul, which returns with them into their new lifetime incarnation.

This is described as karma from a previous lifetime. Some clairvoyants see imprints in the aura, which I describe as karmic markers, allowing them to understand why certain patterns, relationships, and people continue to reappear in their lives and what can be done to understand why this is occurring in order to move forward and end the repetition of this karma.

Famous clairvoyants include Nostradamus and Edgar Cayce. Edgar Cayce's form of psychic ability was unique in that he would go into a sleep- or trance-like state where he was at rest but conscious enough to answer questions asked to him with information from his spirit guides. His abilities allowed him to operate as both a psychic and a medium.

Nostradamus would create a gazing ball experience to go into a meditative state to see his visions. He would pour water or ink into a bowl, which he would gaze into in order to see the future. Both of these types of gazing are still used by many psychics and are highly effective. It is also speculated that Nostradamus used the bowl of water instead of a crystal ball because it was less likely that anyone who discovered him in this state would question it and accuse him of doing witchcraft, which was a punishable crime during the time he was alive.

The Difference between a Clairvoyant Vision and an Apparition

Many of us grew up reading stories about people in ancient times who experienced a vision. In my elementary and middle school years, I attended Catholic school, where I was exposed to the stories of saints. These were people who experienced spiritual visions and received prophecies.

From Joan of Arc to St. Bernadette to the children of Fatima (who saw the Virgin Mary appear to them on a monthly basis for thirteen consecutive months in a grotto), these were accounts of ordinary people who saw extraordinary things.

I'm often asked why there are not as many reports today of people seeing visions as there were in stories from the past. I can't say why for sure, but up until the twentieth century, people took walks in the evening to enjoy the fresh air and often worked outdoors in a slower-paced environment. This pace likely allowed their minds and spirits to take in their surroundings in a more comprehensive way.

Currently, most of the reports of visions come from countries in which people are still engaged in rural activities and are more closely connected with the land. This leads to the question: Does spirit prefer or need a natural setting in which to pull energy from the elements to manifest?

In the course of my work, I've seen apparitions of guides and others from the spirit world appearing before me, which I consider to constitute a category different from a vision. Visions are often mysterious and cryptic in nature. They seem to dictate an order or message. For example, in the case of the children of Fatima, the Virgin Mary appeared to the children, but only when they followed her strict orders of meeting her on certain days and at one location. When they followed her mandates, they were given specific information and instructed only to share the message with the leaders of the Catholic Church. It does not appear that they were able to chat with her about other topics or to spend time interacting with her in any other way.

Apparitions, on the other hand, can appear like a vision with a prime directive, but many times, they also appear and share information freely and are open to talking about a variety of topics and answering questions. There's a sense that they have come to visit, and while they might want a specific message delivered to someone, they are also open to engaging in a less formal and more expressive type of relationship. Many mediums describe encountering both types and often have a preference for which type of spirit they prefer to work with. I grow weary of being just a message taker and delivery person, so I prefer the apparitions who are more social and like to chat. We have a nice visit, and then I pass their message along to whom they wish to have it delivered. Other mediums prefer just the facts; they want the message delivered clearly and quickly, with as little engagement time as possible.

Clairaudience

People with clairaudient ability can hear voices from the spirit world. They typically are also more sensitive to the vibration of sound frequencies, and their hearing is attuned to subtle frequencies. At times they can detect low-level and high-level sounds, hums, and tones from people, animals, and both the earth plane and the spiritual planes. They are great at working with crystal bowls and bells for sound therapy.

Music has a profound empathic effect on those with clairaudient ability as it also triggers their empathic abilities (defined in chapter 2, "Empathic Abilities"). This leads them to attune their psychic abilities to sound frequencies and vibrations from the astral realms.

Many clairaudients report hearing songs and sounds from the angelic kingdom at specific times of the year, such as the holidays, especially the equinoxes and solstices, when the portals to the other side are more open. They also report hearing those angelic voices during sunrise and sunset each day as well as in sacred and natural or man-made locations around the world.

Clairaudients can hear sounds made by nature, the elementals, and beings from the higher planes. Joan of Arc was clairaudient as well as clairvoyant; she heard the voices of the saints and followed their guidance.

One area where I am most attuned to hear these sounds is at the beach, especially during sunrise and sunset. I have also found the winter solstice to be an especially profound time to hear the angelic voices.

The most popular example of a clairaudient is a medium who hears the voices of and communicates with people who have died. Sometimes this communication comes from the earth plane, where the dead are earthbound as ghosts who have not crossed over to the spirit world. Others are people in the spirit world who communicate with the medium from the spiritual planes in order to contact a living person on the earth plane and deliver a message.

Others examples of clairaudience include spirit guide communication, angelic communication, and communication from this world and others with beings like the fae, other elementals, and aliens.

Having clairaudient ability can be one of the most confusing and, at first, frightening of all of the psychic abilities, due to the fact that hearing voices is also a symptom of schizophrenia. While auditory hallucinations caused by schizophrenia are often uncontrollable without medical help, the types of sounds and voices heard by a clairaudient person can be consciously turned off and blocked. Unlike those experiencing schizophrenia, clairaudients don't hear voices in their head of people having entire conversations. A clairaudient receives a telepathic upload of communication, often first heralded by a sound. When first starting to hear clairaudiently, many people describe the experience as a ringing or buzzing sound in their ears. Some hear this as a high-pitched tone, while others describe it like the buzzing of bees. When this occurs, the best thing to do is to relax, breathe deeply, and affirm to the spirit or spirits that you are aware that they are attempting to communicate with you. Then ask them to slow down the vibration of the communication to a frequency you can hear so that you can understand what is being communicated.

To tune in to clairaudient ability, the best way to begin is to engage in a prayerful or meditative space, quieting the mind and remaining open to listen to what the other side wishes to communicate. Many psychics are typically not just clairaudient but are also clairvoyant, so they see, feel, and hear the communication from the other side all at the same time.

Sometimes it reminds me of a text message. You "hear" the beep of the text, which announces that a "message from someone" is being sent to you. You then turn your attention to the phone to read the message. Many times with clairaudient ability you will first hear a sound or even someone calling your name to get your attention. Once you are focused on receiving the message, the larger message is uploaded to you in a telepathic flash, like receiving a text.

Many clairaudients also choose to begin by contacting only one spirit directly for communication and asking this spirit to intercede for them and be their guide so that they can assure that the communication coming from the other side is from the highest and best source. An example of this would be to recruit one of your spirit guides to receive the communication from others in the spirit world and then to deliver this information to you, like a translator of sorts.

The more trained the clairaudient is, the better the communication, as the person learns the difference between intuitive communication with their higher self and telepathic communication between themselves and other entities.

Clairsentience

Clairsentience means to see by feeling. People with clairsentient ability are sensitive to the energy vibrations emitted by people's auras through their thoughts and emotions. A clairsentient understands in great detail whatever others are thinking and feeling privately, as if they were saying it aloud. Clairsentients often make good animal psychics, medical intuitives, and energy healers because they can sense when the vibration is not in harmony, and whether it is in the physical, emotional, mental, or spiritual auric field.

People with clairsentience also feel things empathically because the emotions of others wash over them. They are almost always empaths, who are very compassionate people because they experience what others go through emotionally. They really can walk a mile in someone else's shoes.

I experienced this as a child when I would be in a crowded room, feeling others' highs and lows through my emotional auric field. I would sense their energy in a wave coming at me as they entered the room. Clairsentients have to watch that they do not take on the emotions of others. They have to work to keep their aura clear and protected so that they do not permanently take on other people's feelings. One of the ways to determine if you have picked up someone else's thoughts or emotions is to check in when you are feeling sad and follow this feeling to its origin. Does this feeling actually belong to you, or did you pick it up during that meeting at work, from the store you were just in, or during a phone conversation?

Another fascinating aspect of being clairsentient is how it blends so well with other abilities. Clairvoyants often experience clairsentience as they feel the sense of dread or excitement being communicated to them, even to the point of making them shiver from the cold or manifest goose bumps on their arms. Clairaudients feel the vibration of the communication. For example, when I hear a person's name, I experience both clairsentient and clairaudient abilities as I tune in to the sound vibration of the name in order to connect with the person's energy. Clairtangents experience clairsentience when they touch an item and feel its energy, and clairgustants and clairalients have direct interactions between their feelings and the five-sensory experience they have with people, places, and things.

One of the side effects of having clairsentient ability is that once you have connected strongly with a person, place, or thing, you can easily reach out and connect with this entity for many years afterward. People with this ability can think about a person they have met and feel a string of energy that connects them to that person. Many times a clairsentient feels this energy so strongly that when reaching out to contact another person through their energy—not using a phone or any other type of regular communication—that person will be filled with the desire to reach out as well and will find a way to contact the clairsentient person.

I once practiced this ability after reading about it in an old psychic manual that I came across in my early twenties. I wondered if I could do this type of long-distance communication as a clairsentient. I focused on a person who I had briefly dated many years ago and had since lost touch with, having moved clear across the country. I focused on his energy and sent him a message to contact me.

Within three days, he located me and called me. He had no idea where to look, as neither my family nor I lived in the area where we had originally met, and I had an unlisted number. (This was before the Internet or cell phones.)

When I asked him why he had called me after all these years, he said that I kept popping into his thoughts when he was awake and into his dreams while he slept. He followed this feeling to find a way to connect with me. He called several friends until he connected with one that had my number.

If you have clairsentient abilities, it is important to be careful about where you focus your energy and thoughts in order to avoid unintentionally influencing others.

Clairtangency

Clairtangency is the ability to read an object psychically by touching it. The most popular name for it is psychometry.

Many psychics use psychometry in their work. For example, holding an item that belongs to a missing person can help the psychic tune in to this person's energy and follow the energy lines to where they are currently located.

Most clairtangent people need to touch the person, place, or thing to fully engage their abilities and connect with what is going on within the energy vibrations surrounding the body or object.

They can touch or hold an object and connect with the energy of a person they have never even met or seen. Holding an object that has been worn for a long time is typically the easiest to work with for psychometry. Some of the easiest items to read include a wedding ring, watch, or other jewelry. Antique furniture that has been in a home for a very long time also can hold this energy, as can clothing and quilts.

You can also touch and read the energy of a building, car, plane, boat, or anything humans have spent time inside or on.

Clairtangents can find it difficult to wear used clothing or jewelry or to have used or antique furniture in their home unless these items have either been cleared of energy or are filled with positive energy from the previous owner. Having an item in the home that resonates with negative energy will irritate a clairtangent. They tend to avoid that object, or if the energy is very strong, they will avoid the entire room. They can also find it difficult to be in a crowded area like a concert venue or a shopping mall.

I first discovered my ability when I held my grandmother's watch as a child. I held her watch on my hand, and the energy showed me what I would describe as a small movie clip. In this short movie, I saw my grandmother and grandfather in a very romantic situation. I shared what I saw through pyschometry with my grandmother, much to her embarrassment. Not all objects hold this amount of energy, but jewelry that is worn on the body on a daily basis, like a wedding ring or watch, will tend to store energy that it receives often. If the jewelry is worn during an especially emotional event, it can burn an energy imprint onto the object that can be easily detected. Because of this, I'm very selective about the items I bring into my home if they are antiques. I could never collect antique items like swords from old wars, for example. Between my psychometric abilities and my empathic abilities, I would pick up on these battle scenes over and over, which would not be particularly appetizing in my home or office.

Claircognizance

Claircognizance includes precognition and retrocognition. "Pre-" indicates knowledge of something before it occurs, and "retro-" signifies knowledge of something from the past that the person would not normally know.

The biggest difference between being clairvoyant and being claircognizant is that many clairvoyants see a vision of the situation, whereas many claircognizants describe their ability as "knowing" or having the information suddenly uploaded into their thoughts.

As a clairvoyant, I often describe what I see as similar to watching a movie around a person that tells me something about their life. Many times these "movies" are what I describe as karmic markers, emitting information that has been stored in the akashic records, carried back by the soul, and placed in the person's aura. These karmic markers are in the aura to attract a certain experience to return again to the soul in the current lifetime. Sometimes these markers include people from past lives who are "destined" to meet the person again through what will feel like an "attraction." Other markers send out a beacon of energy to attract a certain situation or even a longing or desire to be something, to create something, or travel to a certain location in order for the soul to have the intended experience.

Claircognizance is like an instant inner knowing or gut feeling of that same information but without the clairvoyant "psychic movie" to explain the reasons why. Some people call it a hunch or gut instinct.

An example is meeting someone for the first time, not knowing anything about them, and automatically not trusting them or having a bad feeling about them. You have absolutely no evidence to back up your feelings, as they haven't said or done anything wrong. You just have a strong feeling that they are not being honest, are being deceitful in their dealings, or are just up to no good.

Most everyone can recount a feeling of claircognizance in their life. We sometimes even call this a first impression. If you think back to your first impressions of people, you will find that you were right most of the time. We have been trained to not judge people by these impressions, and so we look past these initial feelings, sometimes because we really want to like this person and give them the benefit of the doubt. Being open minded like this is a very good thing, but it's also wise to pay attention when you get a very strong first impression that something is off or wrong. It may simply be that there is something going on with the person that you can help them with. In these cases, you are picking up on the energy surrounding them in their aura, which is not their true energy but rather a reflection of a certain situation that is currently causing them to emit this type of energy. Once that situation is resolved, their true energy returns, and it may be very bright and positive. The more you tune in and practice psychically, the better you will become at reading these energy fields and discerning whether or not the emitted energy is the true nature of this soul or a temporary energy blast from being upset or troubled at the time. If you discern that it is their true nature, you may still choose to ignore this intuitive information, only to find out later that it would have been wise to have listened to your intuitive side all along.

Clairgustance and Clairalience

Both clairgustance and clairalience are described as an intuitive ability using one of the five senses to have sixth sensory experience. With clairgustance, a person is able to taste an item without actually putting the item into their mouth. For example, think about eating an orange. For many people, as soon as you ask them to visualize eating an orange, the taste of the orange is so palatable that they begin to salivate and can almost taste the orange, even though their mouth is currently empty. When you think of your favorite food, your mouth may salivate, in a sense having a precognitive moment of anticipating what this food will taste like. Clairgustants can taste many different types of items like this without having the item in their mouth. It's a very fascinating ability, and some positive experiences with it include tasting colors emitting from objects.

This sensation is not always a pleasant experience. I was once working with a woman in an informal energy session when she became angry with me. A man had entered the room to ask me a quick question while she and I were doing energy work, and his conversation with me angered her.

The woman had her hands on me at the time during this energy session, and she transmuted her angry, envious, and jealous energy to me. I felt like I was eating dirt, and the clairgustant impression that came to me immediately was that it was dirt from a cemetery. This woman was literally wishing the man dead, and I could taste it! (This type of situation calls for self-defense: I jumped up, moved away from her, and immediately put up a white-light field of protective energy.)

Clairalience functions in a similar way by providing information about an experience or interaction through the sense of smell. People with this ability can have such a heightened sense of smell that they can smell physical illness in the body. Sensitive clairalients have been able to detect the degree of a body beginning to decay in an area with an infection, cancer, or other serious illness. They can also smell imbalances in nature, like pollution, before they are revealed. Many animals have this ability as well.

Clairalients have been described as being able to smell death on a person, but the smell is a sensory experience that is not perceived through the physical nose. In some cases, I have smelled and sensed decay on a person. The best way I can describe it is that I have the sense of their body drying up and withering away. It feels as if the energy and vitality in their body are quickly dissipating all the way through to the marrow of their bones. The body of the person begins to feel "hollow" as the physical body withers and prepares for the death process.

Whenever I have sensed this in a person, I always psychically see the empty shell of a locust. This withering does not occur for every person as they approach death, but for those who have a very long-term illness, this is part of the process as they approach their time to pass on. It can be felt in a sixth-sensory way.

For some clairalients, there is an overpowering, sickly sweet smell associated with this decaying process of the physical body. The smell is similar to that of a room full of dying flowers. Some compare it to the scent of a Stargazer lily that has become too strong and overpowering in the room.

Clairalients have also been known to smell the attraction between two people, as if they were detecting some kind of pheromones being released.

Exercise: Jumpstart Your Intuition

In this chapter, we've explored the various types of psychic ability. Do you have a clue about which abilities you might have? If not, try this exercise and allow your intuition to be your guide.

Take an eight-by-ten-inch piece of paper and tear it into small strips about the size of the slip from a fortune cookie. On each individual strip of paper, write down the various types of psychic abilities listed above. Fold all of the strips of paper and place them in a bowl.

Hold your hands over the bowl and take in three deep, cleansing breaths. As you exhale, release any negative thoughts or feelings and tension from your body. Each time you inhale, visualize clear, pure, beautiful light energy entering your body with each breath you take. Relax, breathe deeply, and open your heart and mind to the experience. You are opening to a state of grace in which you are interacting with your higher self and with your spirit guides and are preparing to receive helpful psychic information.

After taking three deep breaths, visualize a force field of pure white light surrounding your body. This light is mixed into your aura and creates a dome of protection around you. As you visualize this white light, say aloud, "I am surrounded by the pure white light. Only good comes to me; only good comes from me. I ask that I only receive and engage in what is for my highest and best good. I give thanks." Then ask your spirit guides to assist you as you pull three slips of paper from the bowl.

Open each of the strips and see which psychic ability is written down. Intuitively, which of the three speaks the most strongly to you? Try practicing with each of these three abilities and see which comes the easiest to you.

We'll discuss more about how to work with these abilities in later chapters. For now, just try to tap in and see which psychic abilities are waiting to introduce themselves to you at this time.

Two

EMPATHIC ABILITIES

All of the clair abilities can be taught and enhanced through training. Empathic ability, however, cannot. It appears that one is either born an empath or not, though certainly everyone is capable of feeling empathy and sympathy for people according to their situation. Feeling empathy, though, is not the same as being an empath.

Empaths are immersed in the others' emotional fields, so at times they can feel like they are swimming in an ocean of feelings in a crowded room. It takes time for most empaths to realize that this is not something that others have experienced their whole lives.

When empaths enter a room, they are surrounded by and float in a field of the energy of everyone present. It's like swimming through energy, and the more people in the room the thicker it feels, especially if anyone is upset and emotional. The difference in emotional intensity can range from feeling like being in crystal clear, pure water to drowning in the angry seas or sinking into quicksand.

If unaware of being surrounded in this energy, empaths will just feel overwhelmed by whatever emotion others are expressing. They may find themselves becoming sad or excited very quickly. Empaths truly experience the highs and lows in life, though many times the emotions are not their own but the rising tide of energy expressed by those around them.

It is extremely helpful for an empath to understand what empathic psychic abilities are and how they work. Otherwise, empaths will continue to pick up and absorb this energy, which can affect them in a negative fashion and cause them undue stress.

Many empaths don't know they are one. They just feel overwhelmed being around other people, and some try to escape the overwhelming emotions by self-medicating using alcohol, drugs, and prescription drugs to treat anxiety. (Talk to your healthcare provider if you are struggling to deal with mental health challenges.)

Are you an empath? Empaths have intuitive abilities with the added feature of being very sensitive to the emotions of others or even emotional energy that has been trapped in a room or building.

The following questions are indicators of empathic ability. If you answer yes to any or all of them, you may be an empath.

• Do people open up to you everywhere you go and consider the space around you safe? Are you often described as a people magnet? Are animals and babies naturally drawn to you, and do they relax in your company? Wherever you go, are people attracted to you? Do they feel comfortable around you, like they know you, even when it's the first time they've met you? After an encounter with an empath, most people walk away surprised to have found themselves opening up and sharing their deepest thoughts, fears, and secrets to this stranger. When they are done, they walk away in a daze, shocked that they opened up in this way but feel better by having done so.

• Do you have more intense emotional reactions to television shows and movies than others who are watching the same shows? Does watching or reading the news depress or overwhelm you at times? It's very difficult for an empath to see anyone or anything being hurt, and it doesn't have to be in person. Seeing a photo of cruelty or watching it portrayed in movies or on television is very painful to someone with empathic abilities.

• Do you tend to have a wide variety of friends from all walks of life, being able to see the good in each of them, even when their lifestyles do not match yours?

• Do you tend to describe experiences by how they feel, such as a blue Monday or a snuggly Sunday morning? Do you "feel" fall coming or sense "magic" in the air?

• Do you develop stomachaches or other flu-like illnesses that come on quickly yet don't have traditional accompanying symptoms, like a high fever? Have you been around someone who is ill and began to take on their pains, aches, or illness out of sympathy? Empaths can develop physical manifestations of others' illnesses if they are not careful about what they absorb. They can also become ill often if they are not able to release the toxic energy from others that they are absorbing.

• Do you wake up feeling great, head out to run errands, and find that you feel exhausted and overwhelmed after only a short time of being at the mall or in a crowded store? Or do you find that you've been out somewhere and now find yourself anxious, worried, or depressed, but when you stop to ask yourself why, you cannot find the source or reason?

- Empaths aren't always psychics, but they all have some level of intuitive ability. Are you very attuned to déjà vu, and do you have very detailed and emotional dreams? Empaths can sense at times that something bad may be about to happen to a person, but they don't always have precognition of what actually will occur.

- Do you know what people are truly feeling, even when they are trying to hide it? Can you feel their emotions and the truth of what they are saying, even when they are lying to you or others directly? Most empaths have to deal with knowing the true intention and energy that others are emitting, even though it may be hidden under a façade.

- Have you been described as a healer in some way? Some empaths are naturally drawn to physical healing, while others do what is described as soul healing. Empaths have the ability to take away pain in one form or another. Trained empaths know how to do this without causing harm to themselves. Untrained empaths often take on the pain, causing themselves undue stress and trauma.

- Are you sensitive to your environment, whether it's crowded or not? For example, I can pick up on the local consciousness energy at 5 p.m. on a Friday when the rush of excitement is released as people rejoice when leaving work for the weekend. Does having a routine at work feel imprisoning to you? Most empaths tend to be drawn to more creative lines of work in which they can create their own hours and schedules. Empaths have to feel free and don't do well in confining environments or in a strict routine. It's difficult for them to work in a cubicle all day or in a restrictive environment. They learn better by absorbing and feeling the experience rather than by rote memorization. They are the true definition of a free spirit.

- Do you find that some places have bad energy, while others are warm and welcoming? Are you uncomfortable staying in a place that doesn't feel right to you, when others are not bothered by the energy of a space at all?

- Are you sensitive to used furniture, antiques, and estate jewelry? Most empaths can sense the energy in tangible items like this that hold a lot of energy absorbed from years in a home or being worn by the owner. Do cluttered spaces bother you and make it hard for you to focus and work? Most empaths need calm and serene surroundings in order to recharge their energy.

- Is your alone time important to you? Do you feel the need to pull away and be reclusive for a while in order to recharge your batteries and feel restored? Empaths find great solace in nature of some kind, whether it be the beach, mountains, or forest. They might also need time alone doing one of their favorite activities in order to recuperate after being in large crowds.

- Does seeing people unhappy really bother you? No one likes to see another person suffering or feeling unhappy, but empaths feel physical pain as a result. If they can do something to help the person, they feel compelled to do so. If empaths have an interaction with a person and feel that they caused the person suffering or discomfort in some way, it haunts empaths until they can find a way to make the person feel better.

• Do you have a deep understanding and compassion for humanity? Do you understand that many times when people act out in a negative way, they are expressing their deepest fears? This understanding allows you to continue to love the person while not approving or accepting their actions. The empath understands that while the person is directing angry energy toward the empath or another person, the energy is truly a reflection about what the person is experiencing internally.

How to Process and Release Empathic Feelings

Empaths feel the emotions of every person they are around. They may not even like the person whose emotions they are feeling or care what is going on in a particular circumstance or argument. They may completely disagree with the person who is emitting energy, but they still feel all of the associated emotions. They don't have a choice to care or not to care, though in general most empaths are very sympathetic and caring and deeply want to help people feel better.

People with empathic ability seem to be born with it rather than gaining it during their life. It appears that having an empathic nature is some type of genetic trait that some people carry. Born an empath, I found the flood of others' emotional energy very difficult to deal with as a child; it was overwhelming to discern which emotions belonged to others and which were mine. Over time, I would compare people's energy emissions to different types of music. For example, my mother was an artist and very emotional person, and I always felt all of her emotional intensity both around her and in our home. When she would be very excited, the energy would burst out of her in high notes, like jazz. On the other end of the spectrum, my grandmother was a very low-energy person who rarely showed any emotion. Her energy would play out more like a somber tone by Beethoven during a discussion.

Can you see how clairaudient ability is experienced in almost all psychic abilities? As an empath, I sense the different type of music expressed energetically by each person through their aura. I've often been able to accurately describe which people in a group get along better than others by tuning in to the sound vibration and musical emanations expressed in their aura and seeing which two or three people are harmonizing to the same type of musical notes. In the description of my mother and grandmother above, their energetic vibrations were extremely different. My mother and grandmother had a great deal of difficulty communicating with each other; they didn't seem to understand each other's language. Their harmonic energy vibrations were so opposing that it was hard for them to understand what the other person was saying or feeling. It's like introducing a hard-core heavy metal music lover to someone who loves country ballads. Energetically, they don't often see eye to eye on things, and this can cause conflict. I often explain this in consultations with clients when they ask me why they have difficulty connecting and communicating with another person in their life. If the person does not find a way to speak the other person's language, conflict becomes the standard protocol in that relationship.

The most interesting thing about being an empath is that you gain a deeper understanding of each person as you see how they process thoughts and information emotionally. You see the buildup of emotions of people who tend to fly off the handle or have a short fuse. You can feel it, and if you can see auras, you see the energy buildup in the emotional body of the aura. If a person doesn't like to express their emotional feelings to others, you can see or sense the wall as it goes up and they attempt to block their emotions from being released outward, going cold as they freeze their emotional energy and lock it down inside.

You also feel every emotion that a person is experiencing, whether or not they are outwardly expressing it to others. So in a room of people, you feel the man who is seething with anger before it bubbles outward from him, and you can literally feel the woman who has poisoned herself with jealousy, who hasn't yet shared the ugly thought that she plans to say to hurt the other woman in the room. You see and sense these emotions around each person you are around.

When these emotions are directed toward you personally, they literally cut to the core of your being, and you experience a deep emotional and psychic pain.

Many empaths find it difficult to be in hospitals, where there is so much pain and grief. Empaths are born with these traits, and since most of their parents are unaware of why their child is so hypersensitive, they don't receive any training on how to handle this type of psi ability. They also have very little understanding of or compassion for how overwhelming it must be to feel emotions at such an intense level. Those who don't experience this kind of feeling have a difficult time understanding or sympathizing with what an empath experiences on a daily basis.

When I was a young empath, I could enter a room of people and read the temperature of the room by the energy that everyone was giving off. I could tell if my father was soon to be erupting in anger and when my mother was in a state of high anxiety. The energy would wash over me and enter my auric field, where I would experience the emotions that both were emitting. Because I didn't know how to release this energy or what to do with it, it would stay in my auric field. I would gather too much and end up with a stomachache.

Holidays with large gatherings of family were the most challenging. Invariably, I would be so overwhelmed as I psychically picked up all this energy without releasing it from my physical and aura body that I would become physically ill every Christmas. I would exhibit flu-like symptoms and have an upset stomach to the point of vomiting. My mother would put me in bed, lamenting that she couldn't understand how I could get so ill every Christmas.

Over time, I developed the only coping skill that I subconsciously knew: creating a wall of energy around myself where I did not allow all of my energy to be accessed. I retreated behind the wall, keeping some of my emotional energy safely. tucked away and allowing the wall to block some of the intense energy bouncing around me.

There were times when the emotional intensity of everyone was so high that I wanted to leave the room. Since I was not always able to escape the situation, I learned how to put up a block around myself so that I wouldn't have to feel overwhelmed by the energy pinging around me.

In my late twenties, I finally learned how to properly raise and lower my auric shield so that I could learn how to deal with the challenges of the world as an empath.

What It Feels Like to Be an Empath

Emotions are like water. Water is a strong force of nature that can do great damage at times. Think of a giant tsunami wave smashing against the shore. Strong emotions hit empaths just like a giant wave that can emotionally knock them down.

Seawalls are built to protect against waves, but keeping a wall up all the time takes a great amount of energy. It is necessary to do this sometimes, such as when you are under a psychic attack and someone is directly sending negative energy to you. It is important at those times to put up a wall of energy that will bounce the negative energy back to the sender or stop and zap it into nothingness.

Sometimes as a psychic you need your energy fields to be open wide, allowing you to get a clear read on what other people are emitting energetically. During these times, you will feel all of the emotions in the area, and it's important to be able to discern which emotions belong to you and which you are picking up from other people. It's a trade-off as you learn when to open the floodgates and when to close the locks and allow very little to filter in during very emotionally intense situations.

One fascinating thing I've noticed in my years as an empath is that being around rain blocks this ability for a while. It has to be an intense rainfall, coming down hard. Something about this intense natural energy cleanses away the emotional energy from the area and creates a neutral zone during the time of the rain. This can be a very relaxing and restorative time for empaths. I love a good rainfall, and during a storm, I soak in the energy.

Those of you who are empaths know exactly what I've been describing in this chapter, and I'm sure the journey has been much the same for you.

As an empath, you've probably already learned how to put up some kind of shield to protect yourself when the energy overload is too high. If you're looking for ways to release the energy you pick up on a daily basis, you'll find tips on how to remove this energy from your auric field in chapter 8, "Psychic Self-Defense and Cleansing," and in my book *The Awakened Aura*.

Benefits of Being an Empath

As an empath, you see firsthand that your thoughts are not hidden. Rather, they are reflected all around you in your life, and this universal law applies to everyone.

Everything you think is reflected outward and then created in your life. Each person creates their reality in some part. If you are displeased with any portion of your life, the awareness quickly sinks in that, according to this principle, you have taken part in creating and attracting this series of events into your life.

This concept forces the awakened person to take a deeper look at their life and consider what part they played in each aspect of it. This is challenging from the perspective of the ego, through which we've wanted to believe that everything that we have perceived as bad was done or caused entirely by others. We all want to believe that we are good people who do no harm to ourselves or to others. To accept the idea that some of the negative events occurring in our lives are a direct reflection of our thoughts, words, actions, and deeds is to embrace the fact that no one can "make" us angry. Instead, we make the choice to be angry, and no one can make us happy or sad. Rather, we choose to have this emotion.

In some cases, we have brought this karma back with us from a previous incarnation and thusly have attracted these experiences to us again in order to learn and master this lesson and move forward.

When this is understood, it becomes pointless to keep up a wall in an attempt to avoid the experiences and difficulties of life. They are created to help you to continue on your path of development and evolution.

Empaths provide compassion and understanding to others, with the wisdom that this experience will soon pass, which allows the soul to be free to move on to new experiences.

As an empath, you can show others that each experience, no matter how unpleasant, does eventually end, and it ends more quickly when people work through their fears so that they are ready to see and speak their truth.

Ask the person you are interacting with to consider examining their thoughts and beliefs about a certain aspect of their life if they dislike it. Then ask them to make a change in this area and begin by changing their thoughts about this experience.

Transforming an experience begins with changing one's mindset. The person will need to embrace the understanding that each person is in charge of their emotional well-being and how they choose to be affected by each person and situation. We do not have to be who we once were—we can choose to begin anew today.

We are the creators of our destiny, and this choice to be a conscious creator occurs every moment of our lives. It is our decision as to whether it will be done consciously or unconsciously. When this is understood, people can no longer place all the blame on other forces for the situations surrounding them.

To be conscious creators, we must take a deep look at our lives and then begin to change the picture with an overhaul and reconstruction of our minds. This in turn helps us move our focus from preoccupations like worry, fear, stress, and anxiety onto positive energy vibrations of love, peace, joy, and abundance.

As an empath, you can easily sense when others have made this shift. It shows in their aura, and you feel it in their energy frequency. Helping guide someone to understand what is happening to them emotionally and then assisting them in making this shift in their thinking is invaluable in many ways. This is one of the greatest gifts of a person with empathic ability.

This is the path not just of empaths but of all people with psychic ability, as they use the information they are given to help people see what is occurring around them and how they can move forward to have a better outcome in the future.

Exercise: Use Empathic Power to Dissipate Negative Energy

If you are an empath, it's important to get trained so that you know how to deal with and make use of your abilities. What

I'd like to share with you now is a technique that I was taught for diffusing the emotional energy in the room when needed, to the benefit of everyone. If you are in a room where a situation is escalating into a tense situation, as an empath you can help diffuse this energy and slow things down.

When you sense this energy building up, step to one of the corners of the room. Relax your body and mind and take three big breaths. Breathe in to the count of three, hold the breath to the count of three, and then release the breath to the count of three.

Then visualize a white-light protective field of energy forming around your body. (More information on creating this field can be found in chapter 8, "Psychic Self-Defense and Cleansing.") Call in your guides and ask for divine order, divine wisdom, and divine guidance in this endeavor. See the white-light protective field of energy turn into a giant bubble that forms completely around your body. This bubble is filled with the pure white light. As it forms, visualize the color gold also adding into the mix in order to purify the energy even further.

Then visualize your white-light energy field expanding widely as it fills with the magnificent pure, bright, white light intermingled with the warm, gold color. As the force-field bubble builds around you, the glow emits around your body. Now take your right hand and pull some of the light energy from the bubble. Hold it in your right hand. The bubble in your hand is filled with warm white and gold light. Release this bubble from your hand and let it float around the room. As it moves around the room, it grows larger. The light is so bright and strong that its warmth begins to fill the room, and each person is affected by the pure, higher love of this light. The light allows each person to relax in the warm flow of this energy. The bubble warms the room, which then gathers and holds the energy vibrations as they fill the bubble. If people still need to emit their emotions, they are able to do so in a safe environment in this light. By releasing their emotions, they are also able to get the energy off their chest, as the saying goes.

This bubble will typically last between five and fifteen minutes, depending on how strong you make it. When it dissolves, it carries away most of the energy with it, leaving the room feeling a bit deflated afterward. It's important to remember that you must release the bubble from your field. You don't want to absorb this energy directly.

This way, instead of polluting the energy and vibration in the room with anger or forceful energy, the people in the room are releasing the energy and allowing for some healing to come in around their emotional field.

This is the superpower that empaths have. They are able to gather and transcend emotional energy. Empaths, when properly trained, can harness the energy others express, hold the energy in a white-light field of energy, allow people to express their emotions, release the pain and fear creating the emotion, and then allow the emotional outbursts to be released gently. It dissipates into small droplets and is absorbed into the earth.

Exercise: Advanced Negative Energy Dissipation

Here's the advanced technique of what to do after you've filled the room with the pure white light. You should only try this technique after mastering how to work with all of your auric fields and how to work with energy in this capacity. Otherwise you risk taking on too much energy in your fields.

As you build the white-light energy field around yourself, release part of it as a cloud, formed from the brilliant, white light tinged with gold. This cloud is filled with charged energy that you direct to capture any emotions that are headed your way or zinging around the room. The energy acts like a magnet, attracting the distribution of emotions. Once this energy has been gathered from whomever is releasing it, hold the cloud, which has an extended cord tethered to your white-light energy protective field, next to you. This cord is one that you create in the etheric realms. It is not connected directly to your body, and you do not receive any energy from this cord into your fields.

Continue to expand your white-light energy field into the room, sending vibrations of warmth, love, compassion, and understanding. This settles the energy vibration in the room, which allows anyone in the room to feel comfortable to now open up and share what has been troubling them.

Sometimes when a person releases a strong negative emotion, it is directed at a person in a subconscious attempt to poison and hurt them with the energy. When this angry energy is released and hits its target, it also boomerangs back to the person who sent it out.

So the person who explodes and releases this anger sends it out like a lash of lightning to strike another. The emotion rumbles out like hot lava pouring around them. The energy leaks out and fills all of their energy fields in the aura, causing more pain to their emotional, mental, and spiritual fields. Not only is the angry person hurting their target with their angry energy, they are also causing further damage to themselves.

When an empath has been properly trained and knows how to capture this energy explosion when it occurs, it has two side effects. First, the energy does not hit the person it was directed at, so this person does not feel the intense effect of an energy blast. Second, the energy blast does not return to the person who released it, so it no longer returns to damage them further. Instead, it is held in a cloud of white light, where it is being transmuted into small particles of energy until it becomes so benign and impotent that it falls out of the cloud and drifts down into the earth, where it is easily absorbed.

When empaths know how to do this, they can then be open to the person who released the energy if this person wants to talk about it. Because this person has not received the backlash from the energy they sent out, they will be experiencing a new empty feeling.

They are now in touch with a deeper part of their soul that is not masked by the anger. This is an important moment, as it gives this person the opportunity to truly release a deeply seated emotion.

If empaths decide to capture this energy in a cloud, they must do so with the understanding to be prepared to spend the necessary time with this person to help them through their awakening of being back in touch with their emotions. They also should be prepared to help the person get counseling if needed, depending upon the situation. This is not a beginner type of situation; advanced training on how to create this cloud and release the energy should be taken.

There are also times when the person is so volatile or damaged emotionally and mentally that it is not appropriate to attempt to communicate with them or engage with them in any way. Each situation must be handled according to careful psychic discernment and only after years of training in this technique.

In many cases, an empath does not know the angry or emotional person and is just in a public space with people being highly volatile and emotional, such as a work situation or a party.

Here, empaths can create the same white-light protective shield and create a filter around themselves in front of this shield. Think of it as a window with a screen.

The screen allows air to flow in through the window while keeping out pests. As empaths move around the room, they are able to pick up on the energy being emitted from each person, like air through the screen, but the filter blocks the larger, more intense emotions from being able to move past the filter and hit the empath directly.

This filter can be kept up for hours, though not days, and it does take some energy to do so. Empaths will need to rest afterward and recharge their energy, which is done by having some peaceful time alone doing what they enjoy doing most.

After spending time in a heavy, emotional situation, take a shower to remove any sticky or residual negative energy, breathing deeply to release the energy. Then visualize it going down the drain with the water. If it has been a very trying experience, you may wish to begin with a salt bath first, as salt will immediately absorb and remove the negative residue.

Three

Premonitions and Intuitive Hunches

*P*remonitions are one of the most difficult psychic abilities to master. By definition, a premonition is a forewarning, and most people receive a premonition in a dream state.

There are hundreds of thousands of stories from people who have a premonition through their dreams, in which they receive information regarding health issues, warnings of danger regarding travel and accidents, and warnings to stay away from a certain person, place, or thing. Even presidents have shared the premonitions they received through their dreams: Abraham Lincoln dreamt about his death and saw the mourners lined up to view his casket.

Some of these premonitions are haunting in their reality. One famous case is a 1966 mass premonition by children in Wales who didn't want to go to school because of their nightmares. The children had reported their terrifying dreams of being buried alive for weeks before the event actually occurred. A coal slide disaster then destroyed a portion of town, including the local elementary school.

Other people find that their premonitions first come in physical form as a way to warn them of danger. Perhaps you knew someone who would warn of danger coming, saying that they "felt it in their bones." The body is a highly attuned instrument that we take for granted in many ways. It operates on a complex and at most times flawless level as it processes and distributes information throughout the day. One example from wise women teachings says that when the palm of your hand itches, money is about to come your way. If the left palm itches, money will come to you from an outside source. If the right palm itches, money will come to you from the hard work that you are putting into a project.

When we better understand the rhythms and the attunements of the body, we can understand how it provides an early warning system. We often describe sensing danger as the hair raised on the back of our neck, which is an area open to our psychic sensitivities. Many of us can also share stories of when we detected danger around us as we stepped out of a car or walked at night, when no imminent danger could be seen with the eye. We just know that we experience an increased awareness of our surroundings as the body works as a detection system.

There are thousands of stories about people who decided not to take the train or plane on a certain day, those who turned off a road at the last minute following a feeling, or those who decided to stay home rather than going into work that day, and by doing so, all avoided a terrible situation.

Through my work teaching entrepreneur intuition, I've had the opportunity to work with some very wealthy people who recognize that their intuition is a significant part of the "luck" in their financial dealings. They will often describe the "feeling" that they get about a stock that is about to go up or down or the physical pain they receive in their lower back when they psychically know that a deal is not going to work out. They are actually receiving a premonition with advanced knowledge of what will be occurring in the future. This corresponds to Louise Hay's work on the power of the mind in healing, as she explains that lower back pain is connected to money worries and troubles. Some of these financial wizards have unconsciously attuned their body to signal them when the market or a business deal is going downhill. Once they become aware of what their intuition is telling them through the physical signs, they follow these "gut hunches."

Many successful men and women who don't openly admit to following their intuition will share how it was their dreams, their physical aches and pains, or following their gut feelings that led them to the success they had achieved. From this starting point, I am able to show them how to tap further into these feelings in order to see the waves of energy that rise and fall with each decision and conversation. Of course, intuition alone cannot fuel success: they also put in a tremendous amount of hard work. However, they will testify that the intuitive nudges are what brought them over the edge into great success.

In this sense, business intuition can be taught, but premonitions are trickier. The best training I can offer in regard to premonitions is to consciously direct your higher self to be more proactive in your dreams.

"Who is my higher self?" you may ask. The simplest way to describe the higher self is to explain that your soul is much greater than the part of you who is here on the earth plane having this human experience in this current lifetime. Your soul, which is also referred to as your higher self, contains all of the essence of you from every lifetime you have lived. It stores all of your experiences and knowledge. Over the many lifetimes you have lived, you have learned many things and evolved. The soul, or higher self, contains all of this information and remembers each lifetime you've had. I describe the soul as an upside-down pyramid. Up in the higher spirit planes, the large base of the pyramid is where your higher self resides, full of all of the knowledge of you, and the tip of the pyramid points downward. The very tip pierces the earth plane and is implanted inside you, with that tiny bit of your soul inside you through your aura. This tiny bit captures all of the experiences of this lifetime for you. When you learn to expand your consciousness, you can connect with your soul (your higher self) on the higher planes, where you have access to a greater amount of information and guidance.

When going to sleep each night, ask your higher self to take an active role in your dreams. Speak directly to your higher self or, if you prefer, to your spirit guides and ask to be warned of any problems coming your way. Ask your higher self or guide to help you remember what you are dreaming about when you wake up. Keep a dream journal by your bed and each time you wake, write down what you were dreaming about. Over time, through directing your higher self to be actively involved in your dreams, you should become more cognizant of your dreams and of future events.

An interesting note about premonitions is that it doesn't appear that they can be used on a regular basis for personal gain. People may have a lucky feeling that they use to buy or sell a stock, buy a lottery ticket, or follow a hunch that leads them to a successful outcome, but reports show that these people can't create this. In fact, when their focus turns toward directing energy just to make money using this technique, the proverbial well dries up and disappears. People who continue on this path usually find that the energy from the spiritual planes is no longer available to them for this endeavor and they are forced to then pull energy from their aura energy body. If they do this for too long, it twists and distorts their energy into something dark, and they are not able to restore their energy to the same levels. You'll see that a person on this path begins to have serious health problems that most often start at the base of the spine, which begins to twist and inflict ill effects on both the body and soul. Those who specifically know what they are doing in this practice of the dark arts will then become energy vampires, looking to pull energy from others for their dark desires.

Many people in the spiritual world will tell you that the energy twists this way because these abilities are not to be used for personal gain. It is true that it does seem to follow some pattern and natural law of its own in this regard, and it appears premonitions cannot be planned or controlled. A person will have a hunch out of the blue to purchase a stock or apply for financing on a certain day and will be rewarded, but hunches are random and cannot be forced or controlled. People who choose to delve into the dark arts and use magical practices in order to try to wrestle this information out of the ethers to gain control for personal gain soon find, as mentioned, that it takes a serious toll on their mind, body, and spirit. Hunches are great to follow and are given to us for a reason, but they seem to operate more like a karmic give-and-receive bank account balance. The more conscious effort you put into doing your job to the best of your abilities, the luckier you become.

You can definitely be both spiritual and prosperous. You can connect with your energy and the energy of the universe to become successful and wealthy. The difference is that the energy you pull from the spiritual planes is there to help you work hard to be the best you can be, and the natural return is to be prosperous and successful from these endeavors. This is why psychics aren't able to hand out the lottery numbers on a daily basis, for example. There are certain universal laws in effect that are not truly understood at this time, and it appears that these laws can limit the flow and delivery of this information.

Gut Feelings, Hunches, and Psychic Ability

As a psychic, it's very hard to read for yourself. Most psychics will tell you they are not able to predict their own future or clearly see what's coming for them. It's interesting that we can do so well with this ability to help others, yet we cannot see in the same way for ourselves.

For this reason, many psychics have other psychic friends that they confer with in order to help each other with future plans. In other cases, they rely on their intuitive hunches to help them deal with things in their life.

We all have intuitive hunches. Sometimes I describe them as gut feelings. You get these hunches when you look at a person and just don't get a good feeling about them, or when you just "know" not to take that job or go out and meet that person tonight.

These gut feelings are very important to pay attention to. As many will testify, hunches are hardly ever wrong. Most stories that people share about their hunches or gut feelings aren't about when they listened to them and all went well, but rather when they didn't listen to these feelings and knew they should have. Yet they ignored them anyway, because they felt sorry for the person, felt silly canceling the event that had been planned with other people, or didn't want to hear the fallout and complaints.

Many times my intuitive hunches help me make a decision about something that is directly affecting me, such as canceling a certain appointment, signing some papers at a later date, or not engaging with a person or situation.

Making decisions based on gut feelings is not always easy or comfortable. Other people often don't understand why you are "changing your mind" all of a sudden. On some occasions, you won't be able to explain why you have changed your mind because it would involve sharing personal information about other people that you are only aware of through your psychic abilities. (There is a code of ethics among psychics that prohibits sharing private information about people with others.)

The best way to handle these types of situations is to pay attention to your intuitive hunch and then follow it up with gaining psychic confirmation on the situation.

The difference between having an intuitive hunch and knowing something to be true through psychic ability comes with practice. With a hunch, you have an overall sense of something, a feeling that something is wrong or that a person isn't being truthful, but you can't quite put your finger on what's going on or what the person is lying about. As you develop your psychic skills, you are able to delve deeper into the aura energy field around the person or group of people and can home in on the details to get a clearer picture of the situation.

For example, when people are first developing their psychic abilities, they may walk into a home and feel a sense of dread and sadness, but have no clue why they are having this feeling. As they strengthen their psychic ability, they are able to connect with the energy field in the room and see that a horrible accident, in which people lost their lives, happened here. They are feeling the residual etheric energy from this incident and possibly even a ghost. Another example is getting an intuitive hunch that a person is lying to you or someone around you. You first get the sense that the person is being deceitful, and many times beginning psychics describe this as an uneasy and slimy feeling that washes over them as the person speaks. Later as they develop stronger psychic abilities, they are able to pinpoint the lie by following the energy vibration as the person speaks, and they see or sense the vibration as it goes negative into a lie.

As your psychic ability develops further with training, you are able to tune in to a hunch and see the thoughts and thought forms or pictures in the aura around the person, which portray the bigger picture of it all. This is not one hundred percent accurate all the time. Pathological liars are tricky, as they believe the lies that they are speaking, so the pictures in their thought forms portray their belief in the truth of what they are saying at times. Another difficulty is that when you are emotionally connected with others, your emotional field clouds your ability to clearly discern what they are saying to you. This is why many psychics find it difficult to read for family and loved ones.

The best way to begin understanding this ability is by following the hunch and then gaining further clarity through your psychic skills. In these situations, I begin by paying attention to my hunch that something is wrong. These feelings can be so overwhelming sometimes that I literally feel it in my gut and endure physical sensations of being ill in the solar plexus area. When I then take the time to breathe deeply, clear my thoughts, and go within to center my energy, I can see psychically what is at play with the thoughts and actions of others and discern why my intuitive self is trying to send me a message and warning of things to come.

As you develop your psychic abilities, you'll be able to move from just having uncomfortable gut feelings and vague intuitive hunches to understanding at a deeper level what is going on with the people around you.

Exercise: Advancing from Gut Feelings to Psychic Ability

To begin practicing this ability, pay attention when you have a gut feeling or hunch that something is not right. When you feel this type of energy, the tendency is to tighten up and go into a protective stance.

However, when we become tense, we close down our psychic ability.

The next time you experience this feeling, first ensure that there is no danger present at this time. Once you have discerned that you are in a safe space and are just picking up on the energy of the person near you who is perhaps trying to push you into making a decision or trying to manipulate your feelings, you can work to open up your intuition.

First, take three deep breaths and surround yourself with a white-light field of protection, asking that only energy of the highest good be allowed to permeate your auric fields. See this bubble of white light surrounding you and creating a force field around your energy body.

Now that you have protected your energy fields, relax. Continue to breathe deeply and become more aware of your surroundings. As you relax and sync with your breathing, you will find that the world slows down around you.

When you are ready, pay attention to the energy of the person who is making you feel uncomfortable and producing this gut feeling or hunch.

Now listen as the person continues to speak. If you are able, close your eyes and just listen. If for polite reasons, you need to keep your eyes open, allow your gaze to continue in their general direction, while not looking at them directly in the eye.

In this relaxed state, ask your higher self to assist you in opening up your psychic ability in order to understand what you are feeling as an intuitive hunch or gut feeling about this person. You will also need to work to detach yourself emotionally from the situation and what the person is saying. Allow the thoughts and images that come to you to flow freely. Just listen and pay attention. Over time, the images and impressions will become clear to you.

When you are relaxed, you are no longer in the protective mode that closes down your psychic sensitivities. You have a white-light shield of protective energy surrounding you. Because you are no longer engaged emotionally in what the person was trying to impress upon you, you are able to see more clearly and use your psychic ability to discern what my teacher used to call "the true meaning behind what they are meaning."

With practice, you will be able to discern what others are emitting through their energy fields with their thoughts, emotions, and words. You will see how their energy can disrupt and affect your energy field and others in the same room. Your white-light protection bubble bounces this energy away from you so that it dissipates into nothingness and does not affect your energy field directly. This allows you to psychically tune in and see what energy is flying around the room. You've always felt this energy, knowing that a person made you feel uncomfortable, but with practice, you'll soon be able to determine what type of energy is emitted and understand the meaning of what is occurring in this exchange.

In the upcoming chapters, we'll explore psychic protection so that you have a deeper understanding of how to block energy when needed and can safely explore and be open psychically without picking up others' energy at the same time.

Four

MORE PSYCHIC ABILITIES AND PRACTICES

After reading about the intuitive abilities in the previous chapters, you may have realized that you have had experiences that relate to some of the descriptions of psychic abilities, such as both clairvoyance and clairaudience. Typically, we all have more than one type of psychic ability. The trick is to learn which ones you are the most aligned with and then work to develop those abilities to their strongest level.

Beyond the list of the clair abilities, there are other types of psychic abilities and practices you can engage in. Let's explore each of these types and see which resonate with you most strongly. Each one will give you a clue about which techniques you will be most comfortable working with.

Reading Auras

To read the aura is to have the ability to see and sense the aura energy fields around the body, which include the physical energy field, the mental energy field, the emotional energy field, and the spiritual energy field. Some people see the aura and the colors surrounding each field with their physical eye, and others sense the aura through their third eye, which can also reveal colors and shapes.

The aura has been described throughout history by people in a wide variety of spiritual traditions. Hinduism, Zoroastrianism, Jainism, Buddhism, and other traditions describe the aura as the luminous radiation of energy surrounding a person, portrayed through the seven colors of the rainbow. The colors change, contract, and expand around the person to reflect their physical expressions, mental expressions, emotional expressions, spiritual expressions, actions, thoughts, and feelings.

Many artists have depicted the aura of spiritually advanced people by painting a gold halo around their head or an oval-shaped, glowing, white light surrounding their physical body.

Reading the aura can indicate the health and vitality of a person in their physical body. The size and color of the aura can also reflect their mental capacities, their emotional well-being, and their spiritual evolution and journey. When I read the aura of a person, I see the colors, shapes, and sizes of each of these energy fields.

Each aura is unique to each person, similar to fingerprints. The aura never stays exactly the same: it shifts and moves according to the person's emotional, physical, mental, and spiritual well-being. Auras, just like physical bodies, change in size and health according to which layers are being used the most.

For example, when I see the aura of a scientist, I notice that the mental aura layer is very wide, open, and often yellow in color, as yellow reflects logical thought and intellect. The mental layer of a scientist's aura is often much larger than the emotional layer, which scientists do not access as often since they use the logical side of the brain for their daily work. In contrast, the emotional and spiritual layers of artists are much more pronounced, as they work with creative emotional energy in order to produce their works of art.

The colors in the aura change constantly according to the person's moods, thoughts, and feelings. We often describe what we are sensing in a person's energy field of the aura when we say a person is green with envy, feels blue, or has a sunny disposition. Many people express what they are sensing in the aura without knowing they are doing so when they describe seeing the pink glow of a pregnant woman or refer to someone as having a dark cloud around them when they are having a lot of bad luck. We intuitively sense the energy in the aura, even when we can't see it with the physical eye.

Reading Akashic Records

Someone who has the ability to travel through the various spiritual planes in order to reach the spiritual realm is described as "accessing the akashic records." These records hold every thought, word, action, deed, emotion, and experience that each person has in each of their lifetimes, storing them in what has been described as a book-like container. The records for each soul are kept from lifetime to lifetime and contain the full essence and expression of each soul.

These energy imprints remain attached to the soul through each lifetime and shape each soul's destiny, karma, and life purpose. The records explain who you are and why you are here in this lifetime. They define the challenges you are facing, the relationships you engage in, and the primary motivations and desires that you are attracted to on the mind, body, and spirit levels.

The ancient Egyptians referred to these records when saying that each time you die, your soul is placed on one end of a scale and a feather is placed on the other. The weight of both sides of the scale is then measured. If your soul is lighter than the feather, congratulations! You have experienced and mastered all that you needed to do here on the earth plane and do not have to return again for another lifetime. Your soul advances to the higher spirit realms, and you begin a new journey into different realms of experience. If your soul is heavier than the feather, then you must return again to Earth for another lifetime to learn more.

The Eastern teachings of karma refer to this same experience. If the soul is heavy with the burdens of karma, then it continues on the wheel of life and rebirth. It returns again for another lifetime to learn what it needs to learn and to experience what the soul has created in its human incarnation, both good and bad. When we have worked through all of the karma we've created and experienced all that we needed to do, we then advance to the other side and have new options for manifesting as our next incarnation, not on the earth plane but in other planes of existence. Some souls do choose to reincarnate again on the earth plane—not because they have to but rather because they want to come back and help humanity in some way.

The akashic records hold all of this information, and karmic imprints in a person's energy field can be seen in the aura. The imprints attract certain people and experiences so that the person can work out their karma in each lifetime. A karmic imprint might indicate, for example, a situation in a previous lifetime in which your personal power was taken away from you in a relationship and, for whatever reason, you were unable at that time to reestablish it. This type of power struggle situation may repeat itself in the next lifetime, with the same person again or with a person with similar attributes, giving you another opportunity to face this situation and regain your personal power.

Psychics who can access the akashic records can help people understand why certain experiences like these are playing out in their lives due to karma from a past life. With this information, they can better understand the experience from a soul perspective and learn the lesson so that they do not have to repeat the experience again.

As we are shifting from the Age of Pisces into the Age of Aquarius, we are experiencing stronger levels of psychic ability with which we can connect with our higher self. One of the most interesting side effects of this advancing age and point in time is that the veil between the earth plane and the spiritual planes is rapidly thinning, which allows us to connect our past, present, and future selves into a simultaneous conscious understanding. Science explains this as moving from the third dimension into the fourth and fifth dimensions. The fourth dimension, for example, marks how time is perceived on the earth plane. This allows us to work through the karma from previous lifetimes while creating a greater number of life experiences within this lifetime.

The good news is that we are not alone in this process. Our spirit guides have been working with us in one of the most important evolutionary shifts in our consciousness on the earth plane. When we understand what is occurring to us on a body, mind, and spirit level and communicate with our spirit guides, we can accelerate this process in a state of grace and conscious magnification of our psychic abilities.

As a person with psychic ability, you can learn how to visit places in the spirit realms, such as the plane of the akashic records, through astral travel.

We are always connected to the akashic records through the cords in our aura, so we can connect with this dimension by focusing our auric fields to this spiritual vibration. This is what I teach my students about the akashic records and the connection through the aura. (I go into how these cords connect in my book *The Awakened Aura*.)

When I read the aura of a person, I see what karmic markers have followed their soul from the akashic records. These markers are imprinted into the aura, containing information from their past-life experiences.

At a person's birth, they are activated and send out a beacon of energy that attracts energy in order to bring a certain experience to the person in this lifetime. An example of this is attracting certain people into your life in order to create friendships, relationships, and, at times, unpleasant circumstances. The saying "People come into your life for a reason, season, or lifetime" can be directly related to these karmic markers: they send out this signal until a particular person of the right energy is drawn into your life and you play out this experience.

Once the karmic experience and life lesson are completed, the energy is played out and the people move on and away from each other. Other relationships last longer, such as the relationship with direct family members, but this is not a guarantee of a lifetime connection either. Many people are born into certain families to have experiences and to finish out karmic markers from previous lifetimes. When this is done, they feel less of a connection to their parents or siblings and have the urge to move away and to create a new life without as much direct energy and interaction with their family.

To describe the akashic records and what goes on in these realms would take a book of its own to write. What I'd like to do here is share with you an exercise that I teach to my psychic students on how to access the akashic records when reading for a client.

Exercise: How to Access the Akashic Records

To begin, surround yourself and your client in the white-light prayer of protection (see chapter 8, "Psychic Self-Defense and Cleansing). Once you have filled the room with this pure white light, ask your client for their permission to visit their personal akashic records. Explain to them that you will be looking at their personal records and not at anyone else's private records, for that is against the psychic code of ethics. Explain that you are not going to pry into their friend's or lover's records, for example.

Once you have received permission from your client to view their records, take their hands into your hands for a moment and close your eyes. Take three deep breaths in and out, while focusing on the energy of your client. Then reach out to your spirit guide and make known your desire to visit the akashic records.

You can now sit back, letting go of your client's hands. With your eyes closed, see the white light and your spirit guide there in the space with you. In front of you both is a white elevator.

Push the up button to call the elevator. Once the door opens, step inside with your guide. Inside the elevator, push the button labeled "AR" for akashic records. With your guide's help, seal the elevator doors with white light and state aloud that these doors will not open on any other level, nor is anyone else allowed to open the doors until you arrive at your designated location at the spiritual plane where the akashic records are kept. This prevents any other entity from the astral planes attaching itself to you and from the doors being opened to any other planes that are not as protected or safe.

Once the elevator has arrived at the akashic records level, the doors will open, and you will step inside a very large, cavernous area. Many people describe hearing lots of voices and seeing many people walking around. I describe it as an enormous hotel lobby, with elevators going up higher than the eye can see. When I visit, I see the lobby and go to "check in," like one would do at the front desk of a five-star hotel. My spirit guide waits here in the lobby until I'm finished reading the records.

At check in, I give my name and announce that I have a reservation to view the akashic records of my client and state their name. I then ask for permission to do so if it is for the client's highest and best good for me to see the records, as it is important to ensure that seeing this information will be a positive, helpful, and life-affirming experience for the client. Within a few moments, someone appears to take me to the Hall of Records.

I've had fascinating visits during my travels to the akashic records. I've attended a grand council meeting with beings of all types in attendance, like a giant congressional meeting. This room held hundreds of beings, and the buzz felt like a beehive as people in spirit talked amongst themselves and then listened to the speakers presenting at the meeting.

I've met beings of many different types in various parts of this place, which go way beyond just the Hall of Records. I've been in areas where healings were taking place, where studies and research were ongoing, and where beings of light gathered to make plans and discuss the future. There is always something new and interesting happening at this place. I don't know how far it reaches, as I'm only allowed access to some locations. Many times I don't even know that I'm going to receive permission to see something new; it seems to happen spontaneously. A guide to the records will say, "Come see this," and show me something spectacular.

When on business, though, in the sense of coming to gather specific information for your client, you'll want to stay focused and ask to be taken to a room where you can view your client's akashic information.

Typically when I am on this mission, I am led down a very long hallway and then brought into a small room where I am seated at a desk. The guide typically waves a hand over what I see as a white wall, and volumes of books appear, containing information about my particular client.

I should state at this point that this is how the records appear to me. I do not mean to say that this is the actual state that the information is actually contained in. The appearance of a private room with a desk and books that I can look through, I think, is created for me. These guides sense that this is a comfortable way for me to view and access the information. I'm sure for someone else it would be presented in a way that is most comfortable for them.

As the books appear on shelves on this wall, I state to the guide that I am looking for specific information for my client pertaining to the questions that they have asked me in the reading. This may be a question like "Why can't I ever find a good man?" or "Why do I have bad luck in love?" or "Why is it that every time I get close to success, it slips through my fingers?" So I ask the guide to pull the book from this lifetime and to pull any books from previous lifetimes that will explain why this problem is occurring in the client's life.

The reason I ask the guide to pull this information is twofold. The guide knows all the information contained in these volumes and can instantly tune in to the information needed, saving time. According to the code of ethics of the akashic records, I am there to view a client's records only to help them answer their question, not to pour through all of their personal information.

Once I receive the volumes with the information needed, I open each book, asking the pages to turn to the specific page where the information needed is located. As the pages turn and I read the information, the books then project a video screen in front of me. I see the experiences that are written in the book played out before me like a mini-movie. I see the client in this lifetime and the situations that played out for them. Then I see their past lives, in which they were with these same people, and how the situation unfolded in previous lifetimes. As I view these mini-movies, I see which experiences created karmic markers that have been brought forward into this lifetime. These markers are not punishments but rather simply part of the universal law of cause and effect.

In the spiritual layers of the auric field, I see these karmic imprints and destiny markers that highlight how and why we came back into being here on the earth plane. They highlight what experiences we are drawing to us in order to learn and grow further as spiritual beings. These markers are the universe's way of helping us learn and grow in order to fulfill our highest and best destiny.

When I can see how this karmic marker was first created, I can explain the situation to my client, who can then understand why this experience continues to repeat in their lifetime. This gives them the opportunity to make a change and resolve this situation once and for all so that it won't follow them into a new lifetime.

On the flip side, after reviewing these akashic records, I may find that there is not a past-life karmic marker attached to the situation that my client finds challenging in their life. In these cases, it is something that is being created in their current lifetime. Many of these imprints stored in the auric layers have been placed there in our subconscious through what we were taught to be "truth" in our childhood. These include limiting beliefs about our health, our capacity for wealth, how relationships work, and how the world works in general.

When we become conscious of these limiting beliefs and awaken to the possibility that we have the ability to change them, we can rewrite our current "life book of truths," as I call it. We can revise our thoughts and feelings, creating a new belief system. These new conscious thoughts and emotional connections create new imprints in the mental and emotional layers of our aura. As they expand outward, they attract new experiences to us as well as flow inward all the way into our cells, rewriting who we are, what we believe, and what we can become.

When it's a case of current lifetime belief patterns, it's much easier to focus on creating new thought patterns and beliefs and reach our desired outcome in a small amount of time. When we understand how to do this, we are reprogramming ourselves at the cellular level. This then interacts with our aura body and resets our internal programming. This can be life altering, to say the least.

Once I've identified where the information is coming from, whether it is a past-life karmic marker or a new creation coming from this lifetime of experience, I close the book and thank the akashic record guide for their assistance.

I am then escorted back to the entrance, unless for some reason the guide feels the need to show me something else along the way, which has happened on some amazing occasions!

Back at the hotel lobby of the akashic plane, the records guide hands me back over to my spirit guide who traveled here with me. My guide and I push the down elevator button and walk into the elevator. We follow the same procedure of sealing the doors and stating that no being may enter the elevator while we are traveling nor will the doors open at any other level than our intended destination, the earth plane, whose button is marked "EP."

When the elevator doors open, I am back in the room in my office with my client. I then relay to them what I saw in the akashic records. We discuss how my client can best take this information and use it to change the patterns that continue to appear in life. This information is very helpful because it allows people to understand the experience from a bigger-picture, multiple-lifetime view, which then allows them not to take the current problem so personally in their current situation. They can see that it is something that has been playing out for a while and that once they resolve their inner conflict, they will no longer attract these situations to their life. The karmic marker will dissolve and disappear once it is no longer needed to attract that particular situation.

I find this type of consulting work to be some of the most rewarding and life-enhancing work that I do.

Mediumship

Basically, mediumship is the ability to communicate with people who have passed on from their earthly body. The people can be in ghost form as earthbound spirits who have not crossed over to the spirit world, or they may be in soul form, having crossed over to the other side, and are attempting to communicate and deliver a message to loved ones on earth. Mediums can communicate with and see those in ghost and spirit form as well as communicate with spirit guides, angelic forms, and other entities.

There are a variety of mediumship techniques. In one display, a medium brings the spirit into the room and has them communicate with noises like tapping or playing musical instruments during a séance. There are mediums who go into a trance and allow the spirit to communicate through to them. Others allow the entity to speak directly through them in what is described as "direct voice," and some prefer to channel, in which a medium opens a direct line to the spirit world and communicates directly with the spirits in their plane, then delivers this information to people they are working with.

Another form of mediumship ability is automatic writing. With this ability, the person goes into a trance-like, meditative state to communicate with spirit and is then able to write what is being communicated to them through spirit. Mediums often are not consciously thinking of the words but rather are a conduit through which the words of another being are translated. Some people have performed automatic writing in languages that were unknown to them personally.

Automatic writing was previously accomplished by placing a pen or pencil in the person's hand in front of a pad of paper. The person would go into their trance state and begin to write. Many people now report that they are able to do automatic writing on a keyboard on the computer in the same fashion.

Examples of automatic writing are not as common these days. In the early 1900s, many people would experiment with this type of ability, sitting at a desk and asking spirits if they would like to communicate with them. They would describe feeling a spirit around them who would often guide their hand to write across a piece of paper. The most popular example of automatic writing uses the Ouija board, which doesn't write down anything at all. Instead, people place their hands on the planchette, and a spirit moves it from letter to letter to spell out a message.

As with all psychic practices, psychic self-defense measures should be used along with psychic training in order to protect yourself and avoid encouraging or inviting spirits or entities from the lower astral planes who do not have your best interests in mind when they are communicating. This is not a beginner-level type of activity.

Mother's Intuition

Mother's intuition is another example of a premonition. The mother receives information, often in a dream in which she physically feels the sensation and pain of the danger involved. There are countless stories of wartime mothers who dream of their sons and daughters in danger and sense their death before the military gives the mothers the official news.

My studies and work on the aura indicate that mother's intuition is so strong due to the psychic and physical cords that connect when the mother carries the child in her body for nine months, forging these psychic ties that bind them together throughout the lifetime. Mothers who adopt children also create these connective cords through the heart chakra as the bond is created and generated from their love of their children.

Couples who are intimate and spend many years living together also create these loving cords that connect and form a strong pathway and network. This allows for intuitive information between the two people to pass back and forth more readily.

We also create cords that connect us with our friends. The more time we spend with them, the more these cords connect us emotionally to our friends. As a result, their opinions and suggestions have a stronger influence on us. This is another example of how Mom was right—we should choose our friends wisely, as we are judged and influenced by the company we keep.

The aura offers us an early warning system about people and events. Mothers seem to be the most adept at this ability. I think it's because once a person becomes a mother, the protective instinct activates in high gear, so the warning system is always on and monitoring every situation for any danger in order to protect the child. We all experience these physical and metaphysical reactions daily in our lives, like when we meet a person and have an initial reaction to them of like or dislike, which is why we have been told that first impressions are the most true.

The problem begins when we stop listening to the intuition that warned us early on. Once we become familiar with the person, their charms and influence sway our opinion, and we disregard or ignore the evidence before us. In retrospect, we can see that our initial feeling was the most true, before we were swept away by their sweet talk. Our mother, who is not swayed by this person's energy, sees clearly into this person and tries to warn us, but too often we don't listen, having already succumbed to their charms. If you're a mother with children of your own, you are already seeing this from a mother's viewpoint and understand all too well.

Science is now discovering what wise woman philosophy about intuition has been saying all along: there is a brain in the stomach that processes input on the emotional and mental levels. We would be wise to listen to our gut feelings and those butterflies in our stomach.

By this time, I hope it's becoming clear how psychic you always have been and that those dreams, hunches, gut feelings, prickly feelings on the back of your neck, and inner voice have been guiding you all along.

Armed with this information, you can pay more attention to your higher self, who has been with you all this time helping you on your journey.

Postcognition and Precognition

Postcognition is a type of claircognizant experience in which the person has a "knowing" or dream about something that happened in the past of which they were not previously aware. This could be something secret or hidden that happened to a person in their past and is now being revealed to them, or it could originate even further back in time in their own past-life experience or one belonging to someone they know. An example of a person using postcognition is a psychic detective who is able to tune in and see what happened in the past in regard to a crime and is able to provide information and clues to solve the crime.

Those who have an experience of postcognition's counterpart ability, precognition, become aware of an event in the future with no practical, logical explanation for how they got this information.

This experience is typically a revelation to the person that they possess psychic abilities that could be developed further. An example of precognition is a dream that comes true, which is also described as a premonition.

Precognition is, in short, what psychics do, using their honed skills of ESP and at times engaging in the use of tools like tarot cards, runes, astrology, crystal gazing, and others.

The biggest difference between precognition and a premonition is that premonitions are usually felt physically by people as well. People who have premonitions wake up with their heart pounding from a terrifying dream warning them of danger to come, or they experience a physical pain in the body warning them of an external problem.

These types of symptoms can also happen with general precognition, but not always. When psychics read for people, they can see the person's future and warn them of the danger ahead without feeling it on a physical level.

Precognitive information can be received by a psychic and shared with clients around the world, many of whom they may never interact with except to deliver that information to them in person or over the phone or computer.

In contrast, a premonition is usually based around the individual who has it or around people the indiviual is very connected with, such as loved ones, family, and friends. Premonitions on a larger scale are usually about natural disasters, like hurricanes or earthquakes, or tragedies, like airplane crashes, which will be felt in the global consciousness. The premonition picks up on the waves of emotional effect that a major disaster of this magnitude will produce.

Another major difference between a premonition and precognition is that the majority of premonitions occur within a short period of time. Typically, most reported premonitions occur within twenty-four hours to one week, with a few rare premonitions indicating a longer time frame. Interestingly, premonitions appear to be set in stone, as if it is destiny or fate that this event will occur and cannot be avoided.

Precognition, on the other hand, can predict the future years and decades in advance, offering an advanced look at what the future may hold for an individual or group, but this can be readily changed through free will. In contrast, people who have a premonition are rarely able to stop the event they are predicting. However, sometimes they receive the premonition in order to completely avoid taking part in the event, thus saving their own lives. An example is changing travel plans and avoiding the accident that is destined to occur, and this goes into the concept of it not being "their time."

Telepathy

This is the ability to transfer thoughts and emotions from your mind to another being and communicate with them in this form. There is no physical speech or sound involved: recipients hear or see the thoughts in their head as the psychic communicates. Telepathic communication can be done between two people, groups of people, people and animals, people and elementals, people and those in spirit (including spirit guides), people and aliens, and many other types of entities.

Some of the most famous studies of telepathy have been done by researchers who studied twins. It appears that twins share a deep connection and ability to communicate telepathically that allows for them to communicate with each other through transferring their thoughts and feelings without having to express them outwardly in speech, facial expressions, or mannerisms. Twins are able to do this consciously, and at other times they communicate or experience the connection unconsciously, such as one twin feeling the other's physical pain, even when each is located in a different part of the world.

Many psychics are drawn to doing telepathic work as they learn to develop their ability to project their thoughts outward through the mental auric field. The most popular psychic work to develop in this field is animal communication. In this line of psychic work, psychics first read the animal, picking up on what is bothering them. Then in order to communicate with the animal, they send telepathic pictures and visions to the animal so that they understand what is happening to them. This is necessary to do with animals, since they do not communicate in the same way using language. Using a series of telepathic transmissions through pictures and visions, the animal psychic can help the animal understand that a family member has passed away or that there is a need for the family to move to a new home, or the psychic can explain a physical illness the animal is experiencing and thus the need to have a vet perform surgery or other medical procedures for their well-being.

Whether or not you want to work as an animal psychic, if you have a pet, this technique can be very useful to learn. For example, when I travel, my dog gets very nervous. He knows the day before I am leaving that I am going to travel, even though I have not given any outward signs of travel. I have not pulled out my suitcase or begun to pack or given any signs that I am planning on going anywhere. It appears that he is so in tune with my thoughts that he has psychically picked up on the fact that I am leaving home. A great amount of research has been done on this type of psychic ability of pets, and one of the greatest resources is Rupert Sheldrake's book *Dogs That Know When Their Owners Are Coming Home: and Other Unexplained Powers of Animals.*

In order to help my dog understand that I am indeed leaving the home for several days, I telepathically communicate to him so that he understands that I am leaving and that I intend to return within a certain time span. The best way I have found to deliver this message to him is to show him a time frame that he understands. I send him the telepathic mental image of me leaving through the front door with my suitcase. Then I show him the passage of time through the image of daylight, the sun coming up, the sunset, a night passing, and then the sun back up for the second day. I continue the sequence for the number of days I'll be gone, and then before the sun goes down on the day I'll be back, I send him the image of me walking back through the front door with my suitcase. This gives him a measured span of time marked by the number of times it is daylight and evening before I return, which is how animals mark the passage of time.

Exercise: Consult Your Spirit Guide and Achieve Your Potential

Now that you have an idea of the types of psi abilities that are possible, how do you determine which ones are best for you? Here's a meditation exercise that can help you find your calling:

Surround yourself in a protective bubble of pure white light. Take three deep breaths in and out, relaxing your body and opening your mind into a meditative state.

In this relaxed state, picture yourself meeting a spirit guide from the other side. This is one of your spirit guides, whose purpose is to help you get in touch with your psychic gifts.

See the guide in your meditation and ask for a reading.

The spirit guide will ask, "What is your question?" Say that you would like to know which of the psychic abilities would be best for you to learn and develop. Then ask aloud, "Which three psychic abilities are the best for me to achieve my highest and best potential?"

Then picture your guide giving a reading to you and offering this information. Maybe they are reading tarot cards and the three cards they turn over list the psi abilities best suited for you. Maybe your guide just speaks to you telepathically and lists which three are the best for you to explore at this time.

If meditation is difficult for you and you find it difficult to connect directly with your spirit guides, try this method instead: before you go to bed that evening, ask your guides to show you this information in your dreams or to show you signs during the day that point to specific examples of the types of psi ability that you should use.

The next day pay attention to your surroundings. Maybe you are in a store and see tarot cards where they have never been sold before. Maybe a book drops out in front of you with information on psi ability, a commercial on TV hints at a word that relates to one of these abilities, or a particular website pops up and gives a hint.

Your guides will find a variety of ways to help get the information to you. It's important to remember that you have to ask for their assistance before they can give it to you.

Five

DIVINATION TECHNIQUES

Once you connect with your psychic abilities, you may find that some tools of the trade will help enhance your abilities. These are often described as divination techniques. These tools can help set the tone and put you in the right space to connect with your higher self and engage in psychic work.

To connect with your psychic ability, rituals can help focus and attune the mind. In every line of work, there is ritual to prepare for the task ahead. Athletes, for example, stretch their bodies before they begin to run or throw, limbering up so that their bodies are in the flow of energy. Writers often have a favorite space to work in, usually a desk that puts them in the mindset of sitting down and allowing their thoughts to pour out onto the page.

One particularly effective ritual in psychic work is to light a candle when doing a reading. This tiny flame sets the tone in the room, announcing that you are calling in the white light to surround you and the person for whom you are reading. As you light the candle, you are focusing your energy on connecting through the veil. The active element of fire represents the flame of enlightenment and the intention for information to come quickly from the spirit world, like lightning out of the blue.

Another helpful technique is to create an area where you will work each day to attune your psychic ability. Some people create an altar. Others use a table or desk for their designated sacred space. In this space, place objects that create a feeling of reverence and connection. These might include crystals, gemstones, feathers, a crystal ball, colorful scarves, statues of deities, a Himalayan salt lamp, candles, and wands. You may also want items that you use in your intuitive work, including tarot cards, runes, photos, and articles of clothing or jewelry that you may be using to tap into the energy of a specific person.

Each day when you begin your work, you are training your mind, body, and spirit in the same way as an athlete. To begin, relax your body, stretch, and then do a series of deep breathing exercises. As with all spiritual practices, begin each session with a protective white-light prayer. Surround yourself and everyone involved in a protective shield of white-light energy.

Once you have relaxed the body and surrounded yourself in a protective energy field of pure white light, you are ready to attune your mental vibrational field to the higher intuitive planes.

A common practice is to gaze upon an object, which puts you into a trance-like state in order to be open to receiving psychic information. This is called gazing, and it stops your mind from running away with random thoughts and allows it to focus. Gazing at a candle flame or into a crystal ball are two common meditative practices of this type.

You now want to direct your thoughts to a specific question and open the mind to move from cognitive thinking into receiving information from the higher intuitive planes. During this time, you are attuning your body and mind to becoming a receiving instrument. You are in passive, yin energy—receptive, allowing information to come through you. You cannot be in active, yang energy to receive this information. You must relax and open the passageways so that the energy can flow through you.

Athletes call this being "in the zone," when their mind is not racing with thoughts. They are not thinking about what is happening around them; instead they are in the "flow," in the now, trusting that their body has the muscle memory to know how to perform. While in this zone, they are simply being. They are trusting in the process that they have trained themselves to do, to be in this flow and operate at the highest level of functionality possible.

When you attune your mind and body to relax and be in the flow, you can then direct it to open to the intuitive fields. This is not different from any other endeavor or skill you attempt to learn and work with. It requires practice, patience, and a willingness to work to get results.

Whether you create a sacred space to work or use an object to focus on like a candle or crystal ball, the key to success with enhancing your psychic ability is to set up a daily routine in which you practice opening and working with your intuitive ability.

Create this routine so that it becomes second nature to you. This is exactly the same way athletes are trained to practice daily so that their mind and body are attuned to the rhythm and design of how it feels to engage in their activity. Over time it will feel completely natural to slip into psychic mode.

Once you have attuned your mind, body, and spirit and have protected yourself, your client, and the area with the protective, pure white light, you are now ready to begin psychically reading.

The following are some examples of divination tools that you might like to incorporate into your work.

Reading Crystal Balls

Crystal balls have been used for centuries to help attune the mind, body, and spirit to psi ability. Using a clear quartz crystal ball is a form of divination also referred to as "scrying." This type of divination can also be created by gazing into water poured into a bowl, a still lake or pond, a pool of ink, or a mirror or other reflective surface.

Divination in this manner was used by the Babylonians, the Egyptians, the Greeks, and people throughout Europe. Two of the most famous scryers of this type were John Dee, the astrologer to Queen Elizabeth, and Nostradamus.

In sacred geometry, the shape, size, and form of each item call forth an action into being. The shape of the crystal ball is a round sphere. The round shape represents infinity and the ability to see energy from all directions. This is much different from using a wand, which focuses energy in a distinct direction, from point A to point B.

When using a crystal ball, you are asking to see the big picture and how it affects everyone in the situation that you are inquiring about. It helps provide a clear understanding of what is occurring in the past, present, and future and on the earth plane and the higher planes. Crystal balls are best used to see big-picture prophecies of this type.

To care for your crystal ball, always store it in a box until you are ready to work with it. After working with the ball, return it to its box and keep it away from sunlight and heat.

Working with your clear quartz ball establishes a personal connection between you and the crystal, so do not allow others to hold or work with your crystal ball.

Ancient wisdom teachings say to always put your crystal back into its box after working the ball or to cover it completely with a dark cloth. If it is a smaller size, it can be placed in a velvet pouch.

The ancient beliefs say that those who know how to work with crystal balls can see through other crystal balls belonging to people they know. They can peer through your ball into your home and office seeing what you are doing, as if using a hidden camera. This is another reason to pack up your crystal ball and put it away after using it—so that it cannot be detected by others.

To connect with your crystal ball, hold it between your hands and focus your energy around the ball. You may also like to charge it for a few hours under the full moon.

How to Work with a Crystal Ball

Wipe the ball with a silk scarf before placing the ball on its stand.

Dim the lights in the room where you are working and light a small candle with just one flame. Place the candle about a foot away on the table on which you are working so that the flame does not reflect directly into the crystal ball.

Surround yourself in white-light protection, asking that only the highest and best energies be made manifest through to you. (See chapter 8, "Psychic Self-Defense and Cleansing.")

Gaze into the ball, relax, breathe deeply, and move into a dreamy, meditative state.

The crystal ball does not form images inside. It works as a clear quartz crystal to help magnify and focus your energy in order for you to see intuitive images from the other planes.

Hand-size crystal balls can be used to connect and communicate with other people with whom you have charged crystal balls for telepathic communications.

Remember, the intuitive ability is within you! You are the psychic wise woman or wise man. You are the oracle; the crystal ball is a tool to help you focus your sixth sense energy.

CReading CTea Leaves

The art of reading tea leaves has long been a practice of divination used by the wise women of Chinese, Greek, Scottish, French, Irish, Eastern European, and Romani origin.

Also known as tasseomancy or tasseography, tea-leaf reading is a form of divination using the intuitive ability to discern the meanings of the leaves and their symbols left behind in the cup of tea. *Tasse* means "cup" in French, and -*mancy* comes from Greek and means "divination."

Best done in a comfortable, cozy, and quiet environment, the entire process of sipping tea is a form of holistic healing that relaxes the mind, body, and spirit and allows one to unwind and take a moment to reflect upon what is most important in life.

Tea-leaf reading is an ancient form of divination that, when done properly with clear intention and focus, connects us with the sacred traditions of our ancestors and the elemental kingdoms.

As spiritual beings inhabiting a human body on the earth plane, we have the ability to communicate with the plant kingdom. As wise women and men and shamans are aware, every part of a plant can be used in various magical and ritualistic practices.

In tea-leaf readings, we talk to the plant (the loose-leaf tea). We ingest the essence of the plant by drinking the tea, and our saliva, which contains our essence and DNA, intermingles with the tea.

The entire act of tea-leaf reading is a magical experience. We begin with the cup, which represents the sacred chalice of the divine feminine energy. Then, using the elemental energy of water when brewing the tea, we call forth these water spirits to activate and connect with our emotional and intuitive fields.

Spirit moves quickly through water, so as the plant kingdom (tea leaves) is heated through the elemental spirit of water, plant and water combine and connect to create an open portal to access the spiritual planes. As we sip the tea and think about our question, our essence (saliva) intermingles with the plant and water energies, and the combination of the three elements brings forth the answer to our personal question.

It is said that through the reading of tea leaves, issues regarding what is surrounding the person at this time are revealed.

This meditative practice brings focus and clarity and, when done properly, can open psychic channels and allow messages from the spirit world to come through.

How to Read Tea Leaves

As with all spiritual practices, begin each session with a protective white-light prayer. Surround the tea, the teacups, and everyone involved in a protective shield of white-light energy.

Use loose-leaf tea that is a small to medium size. If your leaves are large, chop them before brewing your tea. It's optimal to use a light-colored teacup and saucer, and the cup should have a wide brim.

Brew the tea in a teapot and then pour it into the cup. For personal readings, you can pour a small teaspoon of tea directly into the cup if you prefer.

The person who is having the reading should drink the tea from the cup, focusing on their question while sipping the tea. Continue sipping the tea until a little less than a teaspoon of tea is left in the cup.

Then, holding the cup in the left hand, swirl the tea around in the cup three times while focusing on the question. Next, turn the teacup upside down onto the saucer, allowing the remaining water to drain from the cup. Lift the cup from the saucer, and you are ready to begin reading the leaves.

The cup is read from the rim, beginning from the handle and then moving clockwise around the cup. The leaves closest to the rim indicate which events are unfolding immediately. The lower the leaves are to the bottom of the cup, the further away in the future the events will occur.

Leaves close to the handle represent the person asking the question and indicate actions connected to them. The leaves are read beginning from the handle and then moving clockwise around the cup. Leaves across from the handle indicate outside influences by other people and situations.

Gaze upon the leaves and use your intuitive abilities to look for symbols and patterns in the leaves. Each pattern tells part of the story of what is going on with the querent and those around the querent in regard to the question.

Always read the cup first. If more information is needed, you can also look at the saucer for further guidance. A person should only have a tea-leaf reading done for them once a day, and no particular question should be asked more often than monthly.

Helpful Tips

My great-grandmother read tea leaves for a living, and I learned the basics of how to read the leaves from the knowledge passed down in my family. Over the decades of reading the leaves, I picked up some tips that I find especially helpful.

Mercury Retrograde

During Mercury retrogrades, it's best to ask questions that look into the past rather than to ask questions about the future, as communication can be unclear during this time. During the Mercury retrograde, questions should be focused on things to review, revise, reconsider, restore, and resolve. It's a good time to ask questions about healing past situations.

Tea Blends

Give your querent a choice of different teas. The ingredients in the blend of tea also give a hint to what your querent is feeling (or what you are feeling). What ingredients in the blend are appealing at this time? For example, I am currently drawn to chamomile citrus, indicating I am looking for soothing energy and a burst of citrus to cleanse and clarify.

When reading tea leaves for others, you can explain to them that the subconscious choice of their intuition is helping them select a tea that is good for them at this time in their lives. For example, they may choose peppermint tea because they need a boost of energy, chamomile tea to help soothe their nerves, or a strawberry and peach blend that indicates that their heart chakra is opening to new love. The reading begins for the person by observing the tea blend they choose along with the color and style of the teacup they select.

Tea Parties

When hosting a tea-party reading for a group, select several types of tea blends so that each person can select the blend that they need at this time. In addition, provide a variety of cups in a wide selection of colors for each person to choose, but make sure the inside of the cup is white so that you have an energetically and visually clean slate upon which to read the leaves. The color of the teacup chosen by each person can also be read intuitively to see their current state of their emotional, mental, and spiritual auric fields. (Consult my book *The Awakened Aura* if you're looking for additional information on meanings of each color and the connection to the auric world.)

Tea gatherings provide a beautiful opportunity to psychically read the tea leaves for people. Hosting or attending gatherings is also a wonderful and easy way to help teach others to open up to their own natural intuitive abilities, as you can guide them through reading their own leaves in their cups in a fun and entertaining manner. I've done tea-leaf readings for individuals, small groups, and for an entire ballroom full of people, guiding guests through sipping the tea, asking their questions, and then reading the leaves in their cups. I walk around to each table, answering questions and helping people if they are stuck on what a particular symbol means in their cup. People of all ages enjoy the activity and share how much they love tuning in psychically in this way when they thought they never could tap into their intuition.

Reading Seashells and Crystals

Since ancient times, crystals, gemstones, and seashells have been used in magical rituals, energy work, and deeply spiritual practices because their energy provides a powerful impact on both the earth and spiritual planes. Ancient Egyptian high priests and priestesses used lapis lazuli and carnelian for personal work on the body and in the temple rituals.

The Greeks referred to gemstones as the bones of the earth and used them as protective talismans. The Druids used temples made from stone, such as Stonehenge, for their ritual work, and the Romans turned amethyst into goblets in order to ward off the effects of alcohol.

Modern-day energy workers work with crystals and gemstones to enhance the mind, body, and spirit connection and for protection and restoration in the auric fields.

Our destiny is to further understand and explore the mind, body, and spirit connection as we evolve in human form. Many natural items are available to help up connect with our psychic energy through the vibratory power of crystals and gemstones and with seashells, which are the bones of the ocean.

My mystery school is named the Temple of Stella Maris. In Latin, *stella* means "star," and *maris* means "of the sea." The name is a direct reference to the power and connection between the higher planes of spirit in the stars and the intuitive, emotional depths of the oceans here on earth. This is an ancient, esoteric teaching. When you learn how to connect these two realms, your psychic ability increases tenfold.

Reading gemstones and seashells is a form of divination that is similar to reading runes, tarot, or tea leaves. The natural energy from the ocean and the shells provides a powerful conduit to the other realms, revealing the mystical connection to the depths of the oceans and the stars above.

Shells can be used to form protective circles when working in the spirit realms and are an important addition to the creation of any altar, whether for a permanent altar in the home or for ritual use.

The shapes of the shells have meaning and practical uses, which define which shells can be used for protection, love, romance, fertility, prosperity, and intuitive abilities.

How to Read Seashells and Gemstones

Here's the ritual that I teach to my students on how to read for clients using seashells and gemstones:

First, you begin with a starfish. The starfish is placed in the center of a table, and it is the anchor around which all shells and stones will move. The starfish is the portal and the anchor to the spirit world, and it has five points. From top left to right, they represent the past, present, and future. The left-bottom point is what's holding you back or blocking you, and the right is the final outcome of the question.

Create a circle around the starfish using large cowrie shells. These shells create a circle of protection.

Before your client arrives, select eight gemstones that you will use for the reading. Here are ones that I recommend:

- *Clear quartz crystal:* can be programmed for any use or intention, clarity
- *Rose quartz:* unconditional love and self-love
- *Amethyst:* peace, balance, meditation
- *Lapis lazuli:* high-priestess energy, wisdom and truth, communication
- *Green aventurine:* opportunity to create or generate wealth
- *Moonstone:* clairvoyance with the divine feminine, soul retrieval
- *Hematite:* protection, removes negative energy

You can also include your personal stone, one that speaks to you specifically with meaning. You can also consider the shapes of gemstones, such as pyramid, cubic, round, etc. Shapes in crystals can be used to signify what is going on in the person's life, and interpretations of shapes vary from reader to reader and should be understood by personal intuition. Place these gemstones in a velvet pouch.

Next come the seashells. The shapes and types of the shells indicate their meaning:

- *Cowrie:* protection and money coming your way
- *Swirl (like conch or button):* change, new energy, wanting to grow and evolve

- *Clam (like clams or cockle shells):* something has yet to be revealed to you, a gift
- *Scallop (like lion's paw or calico):* time and patience needed for this outcome to unfold
- *Triton:* spirit is at work on this, trust the process
- *Sand dollar:* time to make a decision, no more inaction or analysis paralysis
- *Alphabet cone:* symbol of the akashic records
- *Nautilus:* the golden mean; sacred geometry; connection between earth and spirit planes; balance of mind, body, and spirit

Place these shells into a separate velvet pouch.

When your client arrives, surround yourself, your client, the shells and stones, the table, and the room in the pure white light. Ask your client to focus on a question, and as they are doing this, ask them to pull five stones from the velvet pouch and place the stones around the starfish in the manner that feels right to them. They do not know the order and meaning of each point.

Ask your client to continue to focus on their question and to draw five shells from the bag. The client follows the same process as with the stones, placing them around the five points of the starfish.

Once the shells and stones have been placed, refer to the meaning of each point of the starfish. As you intuitively read each point, delve deeper into which gemstone and seashell they drew and placed at each point of the starfish and how these all correspond. Refer to the meanings of the shells and stones to reveal the answer to their question.

At the end of the reading, bag up the crystals and shells that the client drew. Give them to the client with instructions to pull the shells out of the bag in three days' time after the reading and think about what the reading explained and how the client can make changes for the better. Then have the client place the shells and gemstones together somewhere in their home where they can see the items as a powerful reminder of what they are working on to manifest or transform. If a specific gemstone had great meaning for them, they may wish to carry the gemstone with them daily in their pocket or purse.

Dowsing

Dowsing is an ancient form of divination used for locating items, and many people who swear that they have no psychic ability and that psychic ability does not exist still claim to be dowsers or use dowsers in their work. These people include farmers and oilmen, who often hire dowsers to help them determine where to drill for oil in the fields. To dowse, people hold the stick or rod near their solar plexus and walk across the land. They ask for guidance to find what they are seeking, which most times is related to locating an underground water source, oil, or some type of mineral.

The most common style of dowsing involves using a dowsing rod, which is a long stick or rod that forms a Y at the end, or dowsing rods, which are two sticks or rods that are held with one in each hand. The rods in each hand stick out straight ahead until they sense the water or material underground. When the rods sense the water, they cross over each other, showing the person the area where the water or material can be found underground. The Y-shaped stick points out straight ahead until it finds the water source, and then it moves to point downward, showing where the water or material is located.

What I've found interesting is that dowsing works best when the rods are centered at the solar plexus area. There is a direct connection to the third chakra in this process. In traditional feng shui, a *lo pan* device, which is like a compass that reads direction and energy, is used. When using the lo pan, the reader is directed to hold it at the solar plexus area in order to receive the most accurate reading.

Another form of dowsing is to use a pendulum. In this case, the dowser spreads a map of an area out on a table, holds a pendulum over the map, and watches for the pendulum to change its energy. It may speed up, slow down, or make faster clockwise circles over the area that has the desired water or sought-after material. As the dowser gets closer to the area on the map, the pendulum may drop down, allowing the point of the pendulum to specifically indicate where the material can be found.

This technique can be used not just to locate water, oil, or minerals but also to find lost items and people. The map for this does not need to be elaborate. Simple dowsing can be performed by drawing a map of your home and then holding the pendulum over this map to locate car keys or an item in your home that has gone missing. However, a map is not required for pendulum work. Many psychics hold the pendulum in front of their body, again centering it close to the solar plexus area and then walk around a room, around an open field, or among a group of people in order to find what they are searching for.

Dowsing can also be used for psychic readings. Many psychics use pendulums to determine the sex of an unborn child.

The pregnant mother sits comfortably or lies down, and the psychic holds the pendulum over the mother's belly. Typically this works best when the woman is six months pregnant or more. The psychic determines the factor, the way the pendulum moves, that will foretell whether the child is a boy or girl. The most common directions are assigned in this way: if the pendulum swings in a clockwise motion, it's a girl, and if the pendulum swings in a back-and-forth motion, it's a boy.

Six

PSYCHIC ADVENTURES

Have you ever had an out-of-body experience? I remember the first time I did. It was late at night, and I was sleeping in my beautiful canopy bed. Remember those? Mine was white with a bedspread and canopy covered in yellow roses. I always felt like a princess at night when I went to sleep in my canopy bed.

One night I woke up, and all I could see was the yellow rose pattern on my bedspread, which appeared very close to my face. At first I thought my eyes were bleary, and then I realized that I was somehow looking at the roses on the top part of the canopy draped over my bed! I couldn't understand how I was seeing the canopy from above, but I knew this was what I was looking at—I could see the little toy soldier that my brother had tossed up there and that I had been trying to remove for days.

As I looked around, I saw that somehow I was up against the ceiling of my room. I remember thinking, *I wonder if I could see up on the top shelf of my closet.* As soon as I had that thought, there I was, looking into the closet. *This is cool,* I thought, and I spun around to look at the rest of the room.

As I did, I saw my body lying asleep on the bed, and that freaked me out. I hadn't stopped to consider how I was floating around my room. I had been too caught up in the sensation. When I saw my body, it frightened me, and as soon as I experienced that fear, I popped right back into my body and sat up.

Later as I began to study comparative religions and the concepts of out-of-body experiences, astral projection, and astral travel, I realized what had occurred to me that night. I also began to understand that astral travel is something that we can train ourselves to do. For some people, it happens unexpectedly, like it did for me. Others have an experience like this during a near-death experience, in which they pop temporarily out of their body and watch the scene below them while they are in an operating room in a hospital.

Later when the patients awake after the surgery, they can describe in great detail to the doctors what was going on in the room, knowledge that cannot be explained in any other way, since they were unconscious at the time under anesthesia.

Since those early days, I've gone on to learn how to travel out of my body. My favorite type of work in this realm is traveling to the other side and engaging with the spiritual planes.

Let's delve deeper into these various forms of travel and take a closer look at psychic adventures so that you can determine which might work for you.

Astral Travel and Projection

Astral travel is the ability to consciously leave your physical body to travel to other locations in your spirit body or astral form. Astral travel and astral projection allow us to see and extend our consciousness beyond the physical body. The major difference between astral travel and astral projection is that when we astrally project, we can be physically visible to others. Some describe this ability to be seen in the astral form as "etheric projection."

The most common form of astral travel discussed by worldwide religions is the one that we all eventually experience. This is the journey of the soul as it leaves the physical body upon death. The soul then travels to the other side and leaves the earth plane. Astral travel was taught in the mystery schools of ancient Greece and Egypt so that students could learn to consciously focus and travel in this manner at will. In this way, astral travel is something that can be done during one's lifetime and not just at the moment of death.

At night when we sleep, we often astral travel to the other planes, whether we are conscious of it or not. When we astral travel, our spirit can leave the body and travel to other places both on the earth plane and on the other planes of existence. Our spirit is always connected to the body through one of the cords in our aura, described as the "silver cord," which connects people to their higher soul in the spirit planes through the aura at birth.

During astral travel, when we are aware of what is occurring, we can direct our astral body where we want to go. Astral projection is an ability that you can be trained to do with practice, and one example of astral projection is an out-of-body experience, which is not always a chosen conscious experience. Some people go out of body by accident. Many people are scared when this first occurs to them, and they worry that they cannot get back into their body. They find out though that as soon as they have this thought, they are snapped right back inside their body.

This is due to the etheric silver cord. The astral body is explained as one of the subtle bodies connected by a silver cord that unites the body and soul. The ancient Egyptians explained the astral body as the *ka*, the life force and part of the soul body that could travel outside of the physical body. It remains with the body until the moment of death. This cord, along with two other cords, then travel back with the soul to the other side. The silver cord keeps the soul connected to the physical body. When astral traveling, once a person has the thought that they would like to return to their physical body, the soul is instantly pulled back into the body through this silver-cord connection.

A more advanced form of astral travel is referred to as "mental projection." This is for advanced practitioners who have learned how to control the emotional field of the body and have practiced working in astral projection in the various spiritual planes. They have worked through clearing the lower chakras of negative energy and have clear focus on their mental field. In this state they can enter the mental plane with greater ease and concentration. This travel is more advanced and can extend far beyond the physical plane into the higher spiritual planes. This is an ancient, esoteric wisdom practice performed by masters of this knowledge.

Bilocation is the ability to astral travel to a place separate from where your body is physically located. The difference from regular astral travel is that you have the ability to project the image of your physical body in this second area. The official description of bilocation is appearing in two places at the same time. Buddha was said to practice this often, appearing in his astral form in cities hours before he arrived in his physical body, in order to alert people that he would be arriving in their town soon.

The Catholic Church has records of various saints and monks who were able to bilocate. Three that are well known are St. Padre Pio, St. Ambrose of Milan, and St. Alphonsus de Liguori. St. Alphonsus de Liguori is a famous example of this practice because of the very public figure—the pope—whom he appeared to during his bilocation. He was seen by many witnesses in his physical body in a city hours away while he bilocated to visit with the pope in Rome at the same time in his astral form.

Astral Travel to Connect across the World

When I was studying esoteric wisdom teachings, I had to pass many tests to continue on to the advanced level studies, and one of them was an assessment of my ability to astral travel. In your astral body, you can essentially visit anyplace on the earth and beyond it into the universe and the spiritual planes.

My teacher set a date for the test and arranged for a person to be somewhere in the world. I would need to use two of my skills to pass this test. The first was being able to connect with a person psychically, and the second was to astral travel in order to find the person, learn what they were doing, and report back to my teacher.

The day of my test, I called my teacher. He had made sure this would be what is called a "double-blind study," meaning he had spoken to someone and asked them to go somewhere at a certain time, but that he, my teacher, did not want to know the location or any information about what that person was doing at this time. This way, my teacher had no idea where the person was, which ensured that I could not psychically read him to find out the information. He knew as little information as I did.

The only information my teacher gave to me was the person's name, René. This name was even more challenging, since I couldn't be sure if it indicated someone male or female without seeing the spelling. The only way I could trace this person was to tap into the energy of my teacher and find the small thread that connected him to René. I then followed this energy cord until it led to me René's location. This in itself is challenging work. When a person has a friendship with another person, an energy cord is formed. The longer the relationship lasts, the thicker the cord. If this person has a relationship not just with that person but also with their family, the cord splits into multiple cords, which connect them all.

If I wasn't very careful, I could follow the cord to René, but that cord could continue on to René's children or spouse, causing me to confuse the energy attachment there. For example, my teacher could be very fond of one of René's children, and that cord would be very strong and attached to this connection. So it's very important to follow the exact energy cord and be able to discern where each attachment splits and leads.

I traced the cord until I felt the attachment that I identified as René. (This is a master-level technique not covered in this book.) It's difficult to describe how this feels. Basically, when you are working with someone, you have them say the name of another person aloud. When they say the other person's name, there is a sound vibration attached to the name that gives off a specific energetic tone. You can hear the anger or the love or the adoration. This sound vibration attaches to the cord of energy between these two people in their aura bodies.

So I asked my teacher to say René's name three times to me. On the third time, I locked in on this energy and followed the cord. This is the same technique that I use when I am doing a psychic reading for a client. When they mention a person's name, I hear the sound vibration connected to the name and follow the cord until I can connect with that person. This allows for much deeper readings for the client, as I am connected directly to the person they are asking about, even if this person is in the spirit realms rather than the earth plane—the cords stay connected.

So here I was, locked in on René's energy, and I felt confident that I had the right person. Holding on to this cord, I prepared to leave my body and astral travel, following the cord so that I could see what René was seeing.

Within moments, I was standing next to René and could see that René was a man. He had dark hair, olive skin, a medium height and build, and he was walking around in a store. I looked down to see what he's shopping for, and he was standing in front of a vast array of cheeses. The cheeses had little signs in front of them, and many of them were in languages other than English. I looked around the store for clues to my location, and the best I could determine was that I appeared to be in Switzerland. I noted some of the cheeses with the names that I had half a chance of pronouncing correctly and then came back into my body.

I then called my teacher and said that I was ready to report what I saw. I described René and the shop and gave the names of some of the cheeses he was looking at in the store.

My teacher then called René to confirm his location and activities. He left a message for René to call him back. An hour or so later when René returned home from his shopping, he called my teacher and confirmed that at the time that I reported he was indeed shopping for a cheese in a store. I passed my test, and I've continued to develop and explore this ability since then.

In addition to connecting with people on earth, astral travel is used to step out of third-dimensional confines and open the mind and spirit to the other realms. I also use astral travel in my work as a psychic reader in order to connect with the akashic records and access information that is helpful to my clients.

If you're not ready to astral travel, you can always ask for people from the spirit world to pierce the veil and come back to the earth plane to visit you.

Tapping into Psychic Energy during the Solstices

Throughout the history of humanity, we have felt a connection to and reverence for the sun as the symbol of the journey to enlightenment in spiritual traditions around the world. This is found in the high priestess temples of ancient Egypt, the Eleusinian Mysteries of Demeter and Persephone, the esoteric teachings of Mithra, the rituals of the Maya and Inca, the practices of the Druids, the traditions of the Essenes, and the texts from Christianity.

The solar energy is best expressed during summer and winter solstice. We follow the circle of life on the wheel calendar, from winter solstice, to spring equinox, to summer solstice, to fall equinox. This is the essence of the birth, death, and rebirth cycle connected to major world religions and the wheel of life calendar.

The winter solstice, displayed through the path of the sun, is the rebirth of the light within. Stories shared for thousands of years recount the birth of master teachers born during this solstice cycle. Deities and master teachers include Quetzalcoatl, Mithra, Horus, Amaterasu, Krishna, Saturn, Sarasvati, and Jesus, as they are born in the soul form during the winter solstice.

The Celtic cross symbolizes the journey of enlightenment that is formed in cyclical fashion. As we follow the cycles of the year, we move through time in this cyclical fashion, completing the cross within ourselves: as above, so below, and as within, so without.

The rays of light from the sun and planetary bodies affect us as they ascend and descend onto the earth and into our aura body through particles of infused light. This light energy enhances our mind, body, and spirit connection and creates the seasons as we experience the cycle. The solstices, in essence, are portals that when opened allow the soul to move between the earth plane and the spirit planes in order to be reborn. The energy of the summer solstice is releasing the light outward, and the energy of the winter solstice is bringing the light inward. Summer solstice is in the sign of Cancer, which begins the descent to the journey within. Winter solstice is in the sign of Capricorn, which begins the ascent of the journey outward. This is the Path of the Sun/Light. It represents our soul's progression and evolution into awakening our consciousness (enlightenment) through illumination gained from experience along our journey.

If we have conscious awareness of how to engage with these cycles and portal openings, we can raise the energy from within at the chakra levels, which raises our spiritual, solar-fire light.

This allows our energy to rise through the heart chakra and up higher into the throat chakra and the third-eye center. It then reflects outward in order to illuminate and open the energy portals from within. This deepens the psychic connection between our souls here on earth and the higher self in the spiritual planes. During the winter solstice, a powerful ray of light covers the earth, enhancing our ability to receive this light and transform the energy into illumination. It radiates this peaceful and transformative energy. This is why many master teachers choose birthdays around this energy cycle. The cycle reflects the journey of the soul as it begins its descent from the higher spiritual planes down to reincarnating to the Earth plane.

After this peak experience of the longest day of the year, the summer solstice, the days begin to get shorter. The daily decreasing of sunlight represents our journey here through the veil, as we strive to remember our purpose—who am I, and why am I here?

Traveling out of the body during the solstices is an advanced technique. You can begin this process gently by paying attention to your dreams during the day before, the day of, and the day after each solstice. You can also connect with the energy resonating at this sacred time through guided meditations and visualizations during both solstices before moving on to more advanced astral travel techniques.

Pay very close attention to your dreams during the winter and summer solstice, as both will reveal great truths about your journey in this lifetime and what's to come for you in the near future.

CRemote CViewing

Remote viewing is a form of ESP in which one can view a person, place, or thing using the mind's eye without actually leaving the body. Used by both the US and Russian military, it allows the practitioner to gather data about a different location, person, place, or thing by seeing the target in the mind's eye without physically traveling there.

Remote viewers have learned how to home in through GPS coordinates to see if action is ongoing in an area. For example, remote viewers can see if a camp is being built in a particular location, if prisoners of war are being held in an area, if weapons are being stockpiled, etc. Remote viewers can tune in to any place in the world and see what is going on in this location.

The most famous study and work on remote viewing was done in the US Army in a project called Stargate. The people who worked in this program were referred to as psychic spies.

While astral travel can also be used to see things that the eyes alone cannot, the biggest difference between astral travel and remote viewing is that when astral traveling, a part of your spirit energy travels out of your body to another location while attached to a cord that tethers the soul to the body.

In remote viewing, the psychic connection moves through the mental field of the energy body, opening the mind's eye in order to see beyond third-dimensional confines of space and time. The soul remains inside the body during this process. Remote viewing is a technique that many psychics explore—it's like an add-on to their already burgeoning repertoire. Popular uses of remote viewing include looking into caves and mines to see if precious gemstones are accessible to mine and looking below ground to detect where oil, water, and other precious minerals are located in order to drill in the area.

I once attended a workshop on the ability, and each participant was someone who had experienced psychic ability in one form or another. We were all here to see if we could develop our psi ability in the form of remote viewing. That's the furthest that I've ever worked with this particular psychic skill. Here's what happened at this workshop:

The instructor taught us how to remote view by providing a simple test. He placed a group of large manila envelopes on a desk. Inside each envelope, he explained, was a photograph. That was all the information we received regarding the photographs.

The instructor led the class in a couple of deep breathing and relaxation exercises, which warmed everyone up to how the process worked, and encouraged us to use our mind's eye to see the photograph. The mind's eye is not confined by space and time and allows you to see anything, anywhere. It is not necessary to focus so hard that you break into a sweat; you can't force things or try to magically peel back the envelope. Instead, you change your energy vibration and become like the envelope: you speed up or lower your vibration until it matches the energy of the envelope. Then the envelope begins to disappear, and you can see what's inside. With this in mind, I relaxed my body and as I took in each deep breath, I visualized my body becoming filled with light and no longer grounded to earth. With each breath, I could feel my body getting lighter and lighter, as if I were floating, and then, to my surprise, I got a quick glimpse of the photo inside the envelope.

The instructor began to go around the room, asking people what they had seen. He started on the other end of the room and the first reply was from a man who said he had seen something dark with a white light in the middle of it. He thought that it was a cave with a light hanging inside.

Another man spoke up and said he too saw a white light, but he thought it was a tunnel with a light. Perhaps it was a train coming through, he said. Two other women both said that the photograph was mostly black with patches of white.

When the instructor came around to me, I said I saw or maybe felt something different from what the others saw.

I saw a woman and agreed the photo looked black and white. She was mainly wearing black with a bit of white around her head. The rest was what I felt and heard, not so much what I saw.

I explained that I experienced it like a movie clip. In this clip, I heard my spirit guide saying, "She's not really dead, but to everyone else, she is dead." There was an energy about her that said she was not completely dead.

As I said this aloud and tried to explain it further, I became more embarrassed. It sounded ridiculous, even to me, and the more I spoke, the worse it sounded.

The instructor pulled out the photo, and to my surprise it was a black and white photograph of a Catholic nun lying in a glass coffin. She was dressed in typical nun attire, a black dress and a black habit with a white band around her forehead.

"This is a photograph of a nun," he said, "who died many years ago. Her body is kept in a glass coffin, and she is considered to be a miracle by the Catholic Church because her body has not been preserved by any means yet has not decomposed." I would by no means say that I am a remote viewer by trade, having only participated in this one workshop, but I found it a fascinating process to focus on a photo in order to see beyond the envelope. I continue to practice this technique on occasion in order to sharpen my skill set in this area.

Exercise: Easy Remote Viewing Practice

Ask a friend to choose five photographs of various scenes of their choosing and to place each photograph in a thick envelope that you cannot see through. Make sure that your friend picks these photos when you are not around and that you have no knowledge of what types of photos they are. Place the envelopes with the photos inside on a table or desk. At random, pick one up and see if you can visualize with your mind's eye what is on the photograph inside.

Lucid Dreaming

I've had dreams throughout my entire life. Over the years, I've broken them down into several categories, including teaching dreams, prophetic dreams, dreams of the subconscious working through problems you experienced that day, and nonsense dreams caused by having eaten poorly that day, poor digestion, or being ill or feverish.

One of the most interesting things you can do with your dreams is to keep a dream journal and write down your prophetic dreams so that you can track how they come into being. You can also become a lucid dreamer by learning how to be conscious of your dreams while in the dream state. This way, if you don't like the direction your dream is going, you are aware that you are dreaming and can consciously change the course of the dream.

Sound amazing? It is! I remember when I was first taught about the concept of lucid dreaming. I had been so aware of my dreams since childhood and the thought that I could consciously engage with and change these dreams excited me.

I've found that the best way to become a lucid dreamer is to have an active meditation practice. Meditation is key to focusing the mind and developing strong, creative manifestation abilities. During your meditation practice, begin by building a room or space that becomes your sacred space. In this area, practice decorating the room, changing things in the room, and creating new features in the room, like a waterfall, flowers growing, or anything you'd like to imagine. This attunes your mind to being active and engaged while in the meditative state.

Once the mind has been attuned to engage in meditation, the next step is to move on to programming the mind to be aware while in the dream state and to consciously awaken part of you when a dream becomes disturbing so that you can change the direction of the dream. When you go to bed each evening, as you are relaxing say to yourself and to your guides that you would like to remember your dreams and that you would like to become aware in your conscious mind that you are dreaming when it happens. You would like this awareness to gently awaken you while keeping you in a dreamlike state. When you wake in this state during the night, you will still remember the dream.

Now that you have been awakened enough out of the dream to be consciously aware, you can fall gently back to sleep. As you reenter the dream, you will have enough conscious awareness to change anything that you would like in the dream, including having a person leave the dream, changing the direction or tone of the dream, or resetting the dream to be in a different location or to have a different outcome. The changes are only limited by your imagination.

I lucid dream on a fairly regular schedule, and it can be one of the most pleasant experiences to have. The lucid dreamer doesn't fully wake up but just becomes consciously aware of being in a dream. When this occurs, the dream appears to go into a state of suspension. It's on hold waiting for you to decide what will take place next.

Depending upon the type of dream, I may end the dream and say that's enough. I dispel it, and it disintegrates.

If I like the dream, I may switch the location or the conversation so that it is diverted to a more positive experience. From this point on, the dream becomes a very pleasurable experience, and I am the guide in the dream. This is very useful if you are dreaming about a goal or wish, and you can direct the dream to try different scenarios to see how they feel to you. In your dream, maybe you are in your dream house and walk around and see how it feels, or maybe you are trying out a career that you've wanted to break into. This can be very helpful and useful when you awake and are ready to work on a vision board or more creative visualization, which we'll discuss in the next chapter.

Seven

The Logical Mind and the Creative Mind

It's time to find a new appreciation for your intuitive, creative mind. It's easy to see how we've created a disconnect between these two minds: in our modern world, society places emphasis on using logic to solve our problems.

So how do we reconnect with our intuitive mind? Here's the good news: as an entire species we are by nature much more intuitive than we think. We have relied on our intuition to survive and thrive throughout history. Our intuition and gut feelings have protected us when we roamed the plains in search of food and water and had to be wary of predators in the area.

This is no different in modern times. Read an interview with a highly successful entrepreneur or CEO and you'll see that they admit to following their intuitive feelings and gut hunches that led to the greatest successes within their company and personal lives.

The key is regaining balance between the creative and logical mind. Logic is certainly needed when making decisions, but the intuition must come first and be honored as a valuable part of the decision-making process.

Are you ready to open up your intuitive mind?

Vision Board Success through Balance

Creating a vision board is a great way to understand the difference between the creative mind and logical mind and the importance of their balance. Imagine something that you would like to achieve in your life. Perhaps it's getting a new job, finding a new home, or bringing a more loving relationship into your life. Pick one goal that you'd like to work on and place it on your vision board.

Now, you've probably heard about making vision boards before and are thinking, *I know about this. It's called the law of attraction.* Maybe you're thinking right now, *Hey, I've made lots of vision boards, and they really haven't worked that well.*

That's because that's only part of the process of the law of attraction. There is a second component that must be connected to the process, or the entire concept doesn't work like it should. The second component is triggering your emotional field to a heightened state of excitement about this goal when envisioning the board. This heightened state of activity awakens the emotional auric field and tells it to pay attention.

When you first create a vision board, your mental auric field is hard at work, thinking about the goal that you want to achieve. Let's say that your goal is to move into a new career. The mental (logic) field of the aura begins to focus on this goal and outlines the plan of action on the vision board. On this board, you are writing down what you will do to have this new career.

For step one, you will finish the certification needed to work in this career. For step two, you will send out applications and résumés to companies that you feel would be the best to work for in your chosen field.

On the vision board, you are carefully crafting this vision. You have a photo of you looking happy and successful, you've placed logos of companies at which you hope to get hired, and you have a certificate showing you completed the training needed for the job.

You feel focused, and your mental auric field, or logic mind, sees the process and what it needs to do to get you to this destination. It all looks good, right? Then comes step three on the vision board: you place a picture of a check written out to you for your work. It says payable to you for your work in the new career.

As you see that check written out with the large number representing your desired salary, something changes within you. If you are paying attention to your physical body, you notice that you feel a bit of tension, anxiety, and nervousness.

You may have swallowed slightly (or even gulped!) when you read the amount aloud. You may not have even been able to look directly at the check or the number as you wrote on your vision board.

Then you become aware of your thoughts, quietly saying, "There is no way anybody is going to pay me this much for this type of work, nor is there any way anyone will hire me for the position that I want to have."

But, because you are following what you have previously learned about creating a vision board, you push this thought down deep inside of you and continue building the very logical and orderly crafted vision board, which says, "Step three: end result. I get paid for this career."

There. It's done, right? The vision board has been created, and each day you look at the board, read it aloud, and focus on making your dream a reality.

Later, you finish your certification (step one) and apply for a job where you hoped to work (step two).

To your great joy, the company asks to interview you and offers you a position! However, you were offered a different position from the ideal position that you wanted, and the salary is not in the range that you expected either.

What happened? Well, first, I must say that nothing is black and white, so it is not a case of "insert formula here" for an exact result. When creating, envisioning, and manifesting, many variables come into play that may have to do with what is for your highest and best good, including what may be going on in your life and other details that can create a different result.

However, many times when doing this work (provided nothing karmic is affecting this scenario), we can trace the problem back to the emotional auric field—or creative, intuitive mind—where a disconnect occurred.

Back when you were first creating the vision board, the intuitive, creative, emotional field and the logical, mental field (the heart and the mind) were aligned.

The first two steps are easy to align with energetically, logically, and emotionally.

You want to work hard and put in the effort to get that certification, and it is easy to dream about working at a place that you would love. The disconnect between the heart and the mind, logic and intuition, came in at step three.

Somewhere in our lifetime, many of us began to believe that we are not worthy of doing something we truly love for a living. We wrote this belief into what I call our "internal book of truths and beliefs" and placed it into our mental and emotional auric fields.

When you wrote that career description down and posted it on your vision board, you felt the emotional disconnect in your body. It's also pretty likely that you internally thought, *Yeah, right. That will never happen.* This thought radiated through your energy bodies—*that will never happen*—and emotionally you connected with this thought and belief on a deeper level. It might have even comforted you in some way, as strange as that sounds.

Many of us are shocked to discover that we fear success almost as much as we fear failure.

Many of us fear we are not worthy or fear if we were hired for that position, we would later be found out not to be worthy and then would be shamed and maybe even fired. This fear and doubt ripple through our emotional field. The energy in our emotional field is almost always stronger and more intense than the thoughts in our mental field.

While working on a vision board and focusing on it daily, we continue to say, "I will be hired for this position." However, at the same moment the emotional, inner voice is saying, *That will never happen.*

The internal doubt combined with the emotional reaction that we have to these conflicting thoughts ripples through us with such intensity that it overrides the mental thought trying to manifest this number and position.

The intuitive, emotional field almost always overwhelms the mental field. When we are very upset for this reason, someone will ask, "Are you out of your mind?" The answer is yes, at that moment you probably are. When we are very emotional, we fully engage the auric emotional field, and the mental field is disconnected as the flood of emotions takes over the energy fields and the physical body.

The mental field can only truly be productive when the emotional field is in harmony with and connected to the thought that the mental field is projecting. You can say something aloud from a vision board all day long, but if you don't truly believe in your heart that it's possible for you to achieve what you are saying, the conflicting emotional belief is always stronger and will prevail.

The process of using both minds in unison can be seen in all successful endeavors. Athletes who are the champions of their sports describe how they first think about the goal they want to achieve, and then they visualize themselves winning the race or game and how they feel when they win.

They describe how each day when they are working out or practicing, they see themselves winning the competition. They feel the joy radiating through their bodies as they win, hear the crowd cheering, and feel the trophy in their hands or the gold medal placed around their necks. They bask in the glory of winning. They believe that they are the winners, and they can feel this experience emotionally—the joy, the pride, the rush—all before the game is ever played!

Their mental and emotional fields are in complete agreement as well as conscious and subconscious alignment that this goal will be made manifest. They have no doubts about whether they are not worthy to win or not good enough to win. It's just a matter of time before they win. They are winners who are completely mentally aligned and emotionally connected to the win.

Entrepreneurs with a great vision for building a company or product often use the same thought process. They align this mental thought with the emotional impact of their passion and desire to see this product or service coming into being. Everything is aligned to accomplish this goal. There is no second-guessing the outcome; there is just complete alignment with bringing this goal into creation. The passion is awakened in the intuitive field, and then the thoughts of how to create this work take over and bring it into the physical realm.

Returning to the vision board, can you now see how difficult it is to bring this big career goal into reality if the intuitive, emotional field is not aligned with the belief that this dollar amount and new position are accessible to you?

The emotional field overwhelms our thoughts with doubt, which quickly weakens and floods the logical thought energy field.

The next time you are struggling between wanting to manifest a goal and feeling this disconnect between your logical and intuitive mind, don't shy away from the emotions you are feeling and how they are affecting you, even at a physical level. Instead, this is the perfect time to dive into these emotions and swim deep to discover the root core of these feelings. When you can find the source of the emotional doubt and correct it, then you can continue the process to achieve the goal in mind. Use your intuitive mind to take over at this point, and strengthen your emotional field with positive and affirming statements about your self-worth that make you tangibly feel good as you say them. If you say, "I am an entrepreneur who is building a company that will help people around the world," then stand up straight, take a deep breath and radiate this energy from the inside out until you feel your body tingle and a rush of excitement courses through you. When you use your intuitive abilities to connect with your emotional field, you are kick-starting this energy and have a much higher chance of manifesting your wishes and desires.

Are you still struggling with how to awaken and accept new beliefs about your wishes in order to bring them into your emotional energy field? Begin by asking yourself some questions so that you can get to the core root of the problem and eliminate these old belief patterns.

Were you told you were not worthy at some point in your life, and did you choose to believe it? Maybe well-intentioned family and friends told you that your career path would never make you any money and that you would be a failure if you pursued this path.

Were you taught that making money and being successful were not signs of a person who is truly spiritual? Perhaps you were told that living in poverty equals living spiritually.

Find the core of where beliefs like those began and then unravel them.

Here's the trick about changing a belief: you can't *not* think about something, so you can't just ignore it. For example, whatever you do right now, do not think about the Statue of

Liberty. Don't think about how she looks on Ellis Island surrounded by water in New York, don't think about the torch she holds, don't think about what she represents, and don't think about what color she is ... See how hard it is not to think about her? That's what you've been doing when you pushed your belief way down inside and thought it would stay hidden there.

To change an old, negative thought that has become a belief, replace that thought with a new positive thought. For example, when you are working on changing your old thought of *This career choice that I love will never happen*, focus on something that feels believable to you, like *This career choice is well received by many people through all of the hard work I will do in this endeavor.*

Because you are mentioning the hard work that you are willing to do, it allows you to create this new belief—you are already committed to doing the work necessary to achieve your goals and to be a benefit to the company you'll work for.

Later as you grow comfortable with your new thoughts and beliefs, you can adjust them again to grow in new ways. As your self-confidence grows, as you discover that you can handle this position very well, and as you have earned the respect of your coworkers, you may upgrade this belief in your intuitive, emotional field. It may now change to something like this: *This career choice is well received by many people. Ideas flow easily to me, and my time-management skills allow me to complete my work successfully while also having plenty of time to enjoy the fruits of my labor.* In this new, updated thought and emotional change, this thought is not attached just to hard work but expands further as you are able to authentically put your energy into creating what you love and feel confident in your abilities to handle in this new position.

You then can direct the energy into new avenues that you wouldn't have previously considered, including future promotions, profit sharing, and raises. This allows divine order and the highest and best energy to share prosperity with you in ways you may not have considered previously. And, my dear friends, when you are operating in this flow, your creative mind and intuitive field and your logical mind and mental field are truly in balance.

Exercise: Awaken Psychic Energy to Help Manifest Dreams and Goals

Connecting with your creative emotional energy allows the energy to flow in order to help you reach your goals. Once you see how the energy is blocked through the mental and emotional fields, you can work to change your thoughts and to align your emotions with your thoughts. Let's take this a step further and activate your psychic energy in order to help this energy move even faster.

This exercise can be used for any type of visualization that you are working on, such as good health, happy relationships, a satisfying career, or a new home that you will love.

In this case, we are using the example of a new career path. You've created your vision board, for example, and now have worked through any emotional and mental blocks that you had regarding this goal that you want to manifest.

To begin activating your psychic energy, find somewhere to sit quietly and surround yourself in pure white light, asking that only your highest and best good surround you in a bubble of light. Relax and take three deep breaths, releasing any energy that feels tense. Once you are in this relaxed state, it's time to begin psychic visualization.

Imagine a white-light bubble over your head, and inside this bubble an image is appearing of you in your new chosen career. See yourself in this image. You are happy, confident, strong, and full of energy. In the scene, you are involved in your new career, you are dressed for the part, the people you work with are smiling and admiring your work, and the orders for your work are rolling in. Visualize every detail you can—how you look, how you feel, and what success feels like to you!

As you create this image in the white-light bubble, spend a moment watching the scene take place and let this energy fill your thoughts and feelings. Imagine how good, proud, and strong you feel, and think about how exciting it will be to do work that you love and that is appreciated and admired by others.

Once this bubble scene is fully created, bring this white-light field into your aura energy fields. See the bubble above your head and visualize bringing this bubble scene through the top of your head into your crown chakra, where it then floats into your aura.

As the bubble scene enters your aura energy field, visualize the positive thoughts floating into your mental field, the happy feelings floating into your emotional field, the strength and energy floating into your physical energy field, and goals of accomplishment and success for your highest and best good floating into your spiritual energy field of the aura.

You are now activating all this positive, creative, action-oriented energy into your psychic energy fields and filling them with this highly charged, white-light energy.

Each night before you go to sleep, tune in to this white-light bubble scene, which is floating in your aura energy fields. See it as something that has already happened in the spiritual realms, which are outside the third-dimensional confines of time and space.

Focusing on this scene nightly activates the energy in all of your energy fields, which helps it become a reality in the physical, third-dimensional earth plane.

Eight

Psychic Self-Defense and Cleansing

Before beginning any type of psychic work, it's important to be grounded on the physical plane and to learn how to psychically protect your mind, body, and spirit when working in the spirit realms and when opening up psychically and reading for people.

When we open up to the spirit realms, we find that there are many planes of existence as well as a variety of spirits and other entities residing in them. As with all things, there is duality, what we call light and dark, and in the spirit world, there are those who are forces of light and those who are forces of dark.

Some people have been taught that if they choose to believe that nothing bad exists, they won't interact with anything bad when they venture into these planes. I'm all about positive thinking, but having spent all of my life working and interacting with spirits and visiting the spiritual planes, I've seen things. From a practical standpoint, it's like saying that viruses don't exist because we don't see them with the naked eye, yet people catch colds every day from coming in contact with them.

As a psychic medium, I've seen and felt ghosts and restless spirits my entire life. Through my experiences with the supernatural and in the paranormal realms, I've interacted with powerful beings of light, faced beings from the dark side, and seen ghosts from every walk of life.

In my experience, I have seen things that exist that are not interested in expressing love and light, and they do not reside on the higher spiritual planes. There are many different planes in the spirit world, and some of these planes are what are described as the "lower astral planes." The beings that exist there do not radiate the same positive energy as the beings that come from the higher planes. I can try to pretend that they don't exist, but there are universal laws that cannot be ignored. The concept that negative entities do not exist is relatively new and potentially dangerous, as it does not prepare people for what can happen when they open up to the other side. As your travel guide to the other side, it's my duty to share this information with you so that you are able to journey as safely as possible as you explore the spirit realms.

Exercise: Build a Psychic Protection Energy Field

The first step to opening up to your psychic abilities is to review your beliefs, your judgments, your biases, and your fears before delving deeper into becoming a psychic. Should you choose this path, you will need to be open-minded. This is necessary in order to receive information from the other side. You risk blocking information coming into you by attaching your personal biases to it.

Be prepared to see and engage with beings who will challenge your beliefs and what you thought you knew to be true from religious beliefs that you were exposed to in your life. You are on a journey and will be learning the entire time. Just when you think you have figured out how it all works, something new will occur that you never saw coming, and you'll start all over again trying to figure out how the mysterious spiritual planes truly operate. They are not aligned to our linear, orderly, earthly way of thinking: they flow and fluctuate to different vibrations and patterns that we don't completely understand.

Additionally, you will work with many different people in your career who have a wide variety of spiritual beliefs. You will best serve and help them if you come from a place of love and compassion rather than judgment.

Next, prepare your emotional field by working through any fears you have about working with spirit. It's good to have a healthy respect for the other side and to visit with an open heart and respectful attitude. Those who try to demand things from the spirit world quickly find out how this does not go well for them. When you visit the spiritual planes, you'll quickly find out that you are not in charge. However, when you visit, you must have a strong sense of who you are and a don't-mess-with-me attitude. Do not travel to these realms when you are dealing with a physical illness that has weakened you or when you are emotionally upset. Only travel when you are grounded and feeling strong and prepared to deal with any experience that may come your way.

The next step is to adopt a ritual of protection that you should do each time before opening the pathways to visiting the spirit world. I always recommend the white-light prayer of protection, which I've mentioned previously in several exercises. I recommend doing it daily in order to build up a protective shield around the aura. For all spiritual practices, I begin each session with a protective white-light prayer, shared below. In this practice, you are surrounding yourself and everyone involved in a protective shield of white-light energy. Say the prayer aloud three times while holding your arms up in the shape of a V, which represents the shape of a chalice. Creating this shape gathers and holds the energy that you are bringing in around your body.

White-Light Prayer of Protection

I am surrounded by the pure white light. I am surrounded by the pure white light. I am surrounded by the pure white light. Only good comes to me. Only good comes from me. Only that which is for the highest and best good is made manifest through to me. I ask for divine order, divine guidance, and divine wisdom to come through now. I give thanks. I give thanks. I give thanks.

If you are saying this prayer on a daily basis in order to raise your aura energy, when you have finished the prayer, cross your arms over your chest to make an X shape, which seals the white-light shield.

Once you have relaxed the body and surrounded yourself in this protective energy field of pure white light, you are ready to attune your psychic vibrational field to the higher intuitive planes.

This exercise grounds you to the earth plane while also creating a powerful white-light shield that prepares you to open the veil and visit the spiritual planes.

Some people like to call in their spirit guides for protection or wear a sacred and blessed talisman, like a cross or medallion with a sacred symbol placed on it, when they are doing psychic or medium work and when traveling into the spirit realms.

On the spiritual level, it's not so much which technique you choose but rather that you set the tone before working in the spirit world in order to protect yourself before doing the work. This is spiritual protection that every practitioner takes seriously.

On the physical level, it's always best to practice your abilities when you are in good health. When you are ill, your defenses are lowered, and psychic work can put too much strain on the body.

On the mental level, it's wise to be open to the unexpected and unexplained. You may encounter beings and situations that you previously thought were unreal.

On the emotional level, it's best to practice psychic work when you are in a peaceful state. This doesn't mean that you can't be excited and energetic; it means that you are not troubled with other emotional conflicts or dramas that could interfere with you being a clear channel of information.

As I've mentioned, it's always a good idea to begin all spiritual practices and psychic sessions with a protective, white-light prayer. The following white-light orb prayer can also be used to surround a group of people in order to place them into a protective circle and shield of white-light energy. Begin by surrounding your entire body with the white light and then expanding the light so that it surrounds everyone in the circle.

White-Light Orb Prayer

Here we stand at this hour, surrounded by pure white light. Only the highest and best energy is made manifest through to us now. Only good comes through to me. Only good comes through from me. We ask for divine order, divine guidance, and divine wisdom to come through now. I give thanks. I give thanks. I give thanks.

Vulnerability to Psychic Attacks

It's very rare to be the recipient of a true psychic attack. A psychic attack is when someone who has studied mystical arts decides to send a bolt of energy your way in a negative fashion in order to cause pain. It's also relatively rare to spend time with an "energy vampire," someone who sucks and drains energy from others on a conscious level, but it's good to have this information for the rare times that it occurs. Some of these vampires suck energy from others and aren't aware that they are doing it, and this is different from someone who is purposely using psychic ability to harm another person.

What happens much more often is that we aren't properly taught how to ground ourselves before we begin to work in the spiritual realms, nor are we taught how to release residual energy after working in the spirit realms and opening to our psychic abilities. As a result, after we do this work, we can feel drained. This can often be mistaken as a psychic attack coming from someone else, when really we just haven't learned psychic self-care.

The most common problem is working for too long until we drain our energy. We may do too many psychic readings in one day. As a result, our energy body becomes droopy, and we pick up some emotional residue from the people around us. If you are reading people psychically, it's important to release that energy and to do an energy cleansing after you spend time doing readings.

Other times you may not be engaging in psychic work at all but were at a party or large gathering where there was a lot of intense emotional energy in one form or another, and you've picked it up in your energy fields. This can happen even when you are around people who are arguing or engaged in some type of emotional outburst.

Psychic Energy Vampires

Chances are that you've probably encountered a psychic energy vampire in your life at one time or another. When humans take on vampire-like qualities, it is because they have done damage to themselves and cracked open a part of their aura energy field so that their etheric energy is leaking out of the aura. The etheric field of the aura is like the battery that generates energy for us each day. When this field leaks, it's like a car with a leak in the radiator. We can keep refilling the radiator and getting by, but it gets harder and harder to keep the car going.

The aura has physical, mental, emotional, and spiritual layers, and we can create cracks and fissures in our aura through periods of high stress, illness, depression, abuse, emotional trauma, abuse of alcohol and drugs, and other experiences.

If we are not able to heal these cracks in the aura (which is done though sufficient rest, time in nature, time to relax and rejuvenate, and removal from stressful situations), the cracks grow larger, and the energy we hold in our aura energy field begins to leak. We are no longer being restored daily by our aura energy, and this affects us emotionally and mentally. We are fatigued and listless and can become depressed and lose our love and passion for life.

When damaged, the aura tries to repair itself as best as it can, but since it is cracked, it has to continually reach out to bring in new energy to keep it going. It's like a leaky boat; someone has to keep bailing out the water from the hole in the boat to keep it afloat and stop it from sinking. In this case, the damaged aura has to pull in energy from other sources to keep up with the leaking. The closest source is the energy that other people give off through their emotional auric field.

People who are drained of energy reach out to anyone who will give their time and attention. Drained people begin the connection with others by telling their story, their tale of woe, which pulls the listeners in to them. Listeners will naturally feel compassion for these people and attempt to soothe and comfort them, giving off waves of loving, kind, compassionate, and empathetic waves of energy. These waves of energy are absorbed by those in need, which is what occurs with each exchange we have with another person.

This is a normal thing to do, to extend love and care and sympathy. We are energy beings, composed of light energy, and in each moment, we exude energy with our thoughts, words, actions, and deeds. Each moment here on earth, we are constantly creating and exuding energy into everything we do. This expression of energy—thought energy, emotional energy, and active energy—is felt in ripples by all around us.

It's natural to be sympathetic, to listen to a person in pain and in need of assistance, and to offer compassion. This is a good thing, a healing thing, and it is appreciated. When you interact with people who are sad, grieving, or in pain and need someone to talk to, you go through the experience with them. They express their pain and emotions and perhaps even have a good cry. The result is restorative for them. They appreciate your time and are lifted by the experience, as it is helping them work out what they are feeling. As a result, they feel better and get better with some time. This is a good and helpful experience for all involved.

The interaction does not end the same with an energy vampire. The difference between this normal interaction and one with an energy vampire is that the energy given to the person seemingly in need is never enough nor reciprocated.

People with cracked auras never seem to get better or out of this bad mood. No matter when you see them, their tale is a tale of woe, even when the troubled times have passed them by. You see them months later and ask how they are doing, and it is always something depressing and energy depleting. "How are you?" you may ask, and they immediately recite their sad story, with new details added along the way. Something went wrong in life, and they begin to spin the tale, wrapping you in this web of sadness and pulling you in.

When you are able to detach yourself from the conversation, you become aware that you feel drained, as if the life had been sucked out of you. This occurs because an energy vampire's energy field is trying to replace the energy that is so desperately leaking from their auric field. You can never give enough energy to help these people, however. They must stop the leaking from within and repair the damage to their aura themselves.

People with leaky auras will need to get help from someone who is trained to assist them through this negative cycle. This professional can assist them in turning their thoughts around to generate positive energy and life-affirming thoughts and emotions. For most people, this change occurs through therapy or spiritual counseling.

When You May Have Encountered an Energy Vampire

- If you see or sense auras, you'll see the dark gray cloud around energy vampires and the absence of white light energy in their auric fields. You'll also feel the sucking energy pulling at you.
- When you speak with one, you'll sense your upbeat energy immediately fading away, and if you speak to one for more than a minute or two, you walk away feeling exhausted and drained of energy. You'll be tired and want to go to sleep.
- Every time you speak to this person, they always have a sad story about something that is going wrong in their life, and they'll want to dump this story on you in great detail.
- The longer a person has a damaged aura and needs to drain energy from other sources, the more aggressive they can become in stirring up energy. Some energy vampires will create conflict, drama, and gossip, in order to stir up the emotional fields of others. Because people get upset when they hear the gossip or get pulled into an argument, the energy they leak is like an all-you-can-eat emotional energy buffet, which benefits the energy vampire.

- Most energy vampires have no clue what they are doing and would be shocked to learn that they are draining energy from others. They are in a depressed state and are unaware of what is going on with their aura and energy bodies.

Intentional Energy Vampire Attacks

There are some people who have studied and trained to psychically drain energy and do so for very dark purposes. At all costs, stay away from these people. They will attempt to lure you in with what they are doing and will explain that they will share this power with you. This is part of the appeal that draws some people in, yet they find that they are now caught in this person's snare and that it is extremely difficult to remove themselves from this situation. These attackers are predators and have little regard for others.

When encountering an energy vampire, it's important to put up your white-light energy shield until you can remove yourself from the situation. Having said that, it's not good to leave this shield up all the time, as it keeps you from drawing in positive energy during this time. Do not stay around this person for long periods of time, as keeping the shield up for protection can drain you as well.

When putting up your white-light energy field to protect from an energy vampire, say this protective mantra:

I am filled with the pure white light.
My shield is strong; you cannot fight.
Release this hold; it slips away.
White light protects me, here to stay.

If you follow the exercises in this book, they will help keep your energy bodies charged and filled with white light, which will nourish you and keep you from feeling drained when doing psychic work. The white-light energy exercises also keep your aura fully charged and make it very difficult for a psychic energy vampire to penetrate.

Handling Uncomfortable Psychic Experiences

Sometimes a more defensive stance is needed when you're under a psychic attack or caught somewhere a lot of negative energy is flying around. I recommend the following four techniques for dealing with this energy and uncomfortable psychic experiences.

Mirror of Reflection

Turn your white-light shield that surrounds your body into a reflecting mirror so that all of the energy directed toward you is now reflected back to the sender.

Use your psychic ability to locate the energy ripple coming from the person who is attempting to harm you. Once you have connected with their energy, visualize the white light around you turning into a mirrored reflection. Mix the color silver into your white-light shield. Then direct the mirror in front of the energy blast that you are receiving so that it sends the energy back to the sender. This typically stops the attack quickly because the sender receives a blast of energy. This is a taste of their own medicine, as the negative energy they were creating is sent back threefold to them.

This mirror shield is a defensive, protective act, used to protect yourself when someone knows what they are doing and are intentionally sending direct negative energy to harm you via psychic attack. This person means malice toward you and you are taking self-defensive action to put a stop to it.

In a less aggressive psychic attack, you can ask the mirror not to direct the energy blast back to the person but rather to reflect back to the person the emotional and empathic understanding of the damage they are doing with their harmful words and actions. In this reflection, they will not feel the anger they are projecting but rather the emotional and physical pain that is being caused by their act.

In this example, the person is spewing negative energy outward. You may be the target of their anger for one reason or another, but the person is not a trained dark arts psychic attacker. The attacker is just expressing anger, and you are on the receiving end of this negative energy.

In this case, allowing them to see through the mirror image of the pain they are causing to another person, as well as the harm it does to them to be in anger, can awaken their subconscious to stop sending this energy. This can potentially help them consider making better choices in the future about living in anger or letting things go before stirring up ugly anger energy inside themselves.

Protective Shields

You can ward a talisman to wear or keep on your body, like a necklace or crystal kept in your pocket. The best crystal for this type of work is a hematite or a quartz crystal, which can be charged with white-light energy along with the command to repel all energy that is not coming from the highest and best good.

When you feel energy being directed toward you, touch this item and locate the ripple of energy coming from the blast. Send the energy rippling back from where it came.

At the same time, this connects your talisman with the energy as it continues to be directed your way. The energy directed at you is now tethered to this talisman item. As a result, your talisman may take the direct hit from this attack. You will feel it if this happens, as you will no longer sense any energy from the talisman: it will appear to be "dead." It is now void of energy because it has been damaged by absorbing the blow from the attack.

When this occurs, it is time to retire the talisman and create a new one.

Make the Sign of the Cross

In the ancient Egyptian mystery schools, the cross was used as the symbol of the ankh. There are many styles of the cross, the Celtic cross being another one, which has been used by ancient cultures for protection.

The cross represents the body. The piece running top to bottom is the trunk of the body. The rounded area as seen on the ankh is the head, and it runs down through the spine to the feet. The horizontal section represents the arms extended outward from the torso, opening the heart chakra.

In Catholicism, the sign of the cross is made on the body, touching the third eye area, then touching the heart chakra area, and then opening the left and right sides of the body.

Making the sign of the cross over the body in this fashion creates a protective field of light opening this portal from the higher realms. When doing the hand gestures to make the sign of the cross, say a prayer of your choosing to engage with the angels and higher deities on the other side in order to activate this protection.

In situations where the greatest protection is needed, the four archangels can be called in, focusing on Archangel Michael to protect you at this time. This is not something that should be done lightly or at the slightest offense. Archangels should be treated with the highest respect and not called in to help with small offenses. This is to protect you in the most serious of matters only.

Once you activate the sign of the cross and ask for protective help, see the cross expanding in front of your body, growing larger and larger until it covers your entire body and you are glowing with the white light in the shape of the cross. The cross begins to glow with a white-hot light, and the archangels are surrounding you at the four directions—north, south, east, and west. At this point you are filled with the pure white-light energy of the cross, which repels negative energy sent your way.

Less Direct Interactions

Sometimes you don't want to be in a defensive mode. In some cases, mirroring back the energy just further angers people directing it at you. When they refuel and build up their energy again, they are just going to want to send more angry energy at you. Here are three ways you can diffuse this energy indirectly.

Put Them on Ice

Take a photo of the person, write their name on the back of the photo, and put it in a ziplock bag. Fill the bag with water, surround the bag in a field of white light, mix a cool blue color into the white-light shield, and then place the bag into the freezer. In essence, you are freezing their energy and cooling down the negative energy being directed at you.

Build Up Your Auric Field

Say the pure white-light prayer and add a bit of red and orange into the white-light shield. Ask your guides to surround you with powerful positive energy so that the energy directed at you is burned away before it can directly affect you.

This is creating a force field that blocks the attacks from affecting your energy bodies. Think of it as a bug zapper that zaps the negative energy before it even reaches you.

Create an Invisible Shield

In a negative environment, like at a party or family event, where angry energy is flying around everywhere and you can't leave it right away, creating an invisible shield can help you ride through the emotional storm.

What you do is build up the white-light protective shield around you, but rather than turning it into a mirror and bouncing the energy around or directing it back to the sender, which would further inflame the anger in the room, instead turn your white-light field into a thick, white mist around you.

The mist gets so thick and foggy around you that you begin to blend into the background. Your features are not as prominent, and other people in the room cannot easily detect your energy imprint. In this sense, you are becoming invisible in the room and will not be targeted by others when the verbal attacks and emotional insults are flying. This is only a temporary solution until you can remove yourself from the situation.

To do this, you must slow down your energy, breathe calmly, and sit quietly. Don't move around, and, most importantly, you have to relax your emotional field. Don't take in what others are saying; don't focus on their words and emotions. See yourself as a boat sitting on a calm lake as the misty fog rolls in around you. There you are sitting quietly on the boat on a very calm lake, floating in the mist.

Cleansing Energy Residue from Your Aura Energy Bodies

After experiencing a psychic attack or to cleanse your aura bodies after doing many readings or being around a group of people, you may wish to clear any residual energy that you have taken on in your aura energy bodies and restore your auric fields. This is always a good practice; it helps ensure that the energy that remains floating in your fields belongs only to you and that you are not affected by other energy that may have become attached to you throughout the day.

The easiest way to clear the energy from your aura is to take a bath sprinkled with some sea salt, which will help restore your aura and remove the negative effects. Salt absorbs the negative energy from your auric body and washes it away in the water. Take a bath and soak in the water for a few minutes, and then turn on the shower to remove any remaining sticky energetic residue from your body. While in the bath, visualize a pure white light tinged with electric blue that is scanning your body. Any energy that does not belong to you is removed from your auric bodies and you are restored and revitalized.

After your bath, dress in a white cotton gown or T-shirt. The white color absorbs new energy coming from the spirit planes as you sleep, and cotton is a natural fiber, which does not inhibit energy absorption like synthetic fibers can.

You can also dip your talisman and crystals in salt water that you have blessed with the white light in order to cleanse them. A quick dip is all that you will want, as some crystals do not do well in salt water. Check to see which crystals and gemstones can be in salt water for a moment before choosing one as your talisman, as you'll want to cleanse them on occasion. Allow the talisman to dry overnight, under moonlight shining through a window if possible. When you're ready the next day, it's time to recharge your talisman and crystals with white-light energy and a positive statement of what you wish them to be charged with, such as protective energy.

I also highly recommend placing Himalayan salt lamps in the office and home, especially in the bedroom where you sleep. The salt lamps create negative ions, which refresh and restore the aura energy bodies and create protective and soothing energy, which also help restore the auric fields.

Now that you've cleansed your aura, it's a good time to recharge your energy body with positive energy.

Exercise: After-Shower Ritual to Psychically Recharge Your Energy Body

Begin by surrounding yourself in the pure white light. Say aloud in a strong commanding voice, "Divine order: This pure water renews me. Divine light: The rays of the sun nourish me. Divine energy: I am filled with white light as I journey forward."

Touch your forehead and say, "Divine wisdom: Let my mind open to the truth."

Touch your lips and say, "Divine communication: Let my lips speak the truth."

Touch your heart area and say, "Divine love: Let my heart seek the ways of pure love, now and always."

Touch each palm and say, "Divine touch: Let my hands be gifted to work in healing ways."

Touch each foot and say, "Divine journey: Let my feet ever walk upon the sacred path."

You've now done an energy reset on your body and have cleared your auric pathways. You should feel pretty good!

Cleansing Energy in the Home

You will want to energetically cleanse your home often if you conduct readings in your home and even after having groups of people in your home for parties and functions. There is such a thing as "energy buildup," and the more open you become psychically, the more you will pick up on this energy clutter and find that you don't want it clogging up your home.

As an energy reader, I see others' auras and also feel the aura energy in buildings and homes. As we emit energy on a daily basis, this energy is projected outward through what we say and do.

Words have great power. They can be used to hurt, heal, soothe, and destroy. Words are a form of energy, and energy does not die; it just changes form.

All things are made of energy. When we speak, our words have power, and if they are spoken forcefully in an excited or angry way through our auric emotional field, the power is increased tenfold.

With this in mind, how important are our words? Imagine what we are all creating energetically in our aura on a daily basis with our thoughts and words. As these words are released and spoken aloud to others, try to visualize what they do to other people's auras on a daily basis. Words can cut and slice and tear into a person. They can hurt and they can heal. When we blast at another person in anger with our words, we think we are hurting them, but we are also hurting ourselves because that energy blast of anger remains in our auric field as well. We, along with everyone else who hears those words, are hit with collateral damage

Words have a sticky substance in their energy field when their energy is projected. This was a grand design, created so that as we emote what we feel, we are creating. We are creators, and every word we speak creates or destroys. If we look at the Christian creation story, it says that in the beginning, Earth was created with a word—that's some inspirational manifesting power.

This is why when we chant, when we pray, when we speak, and when we bless something with our words, it has great power to prosper, to heal, or to wound. The sticky energy of each word attaches itself to our aura and to the auras of others when we speak to them. This is why if we have been told something negative about ourselves since our childhood that was repeated to us often, it is difficult to detach from this energy. It has built up over time into a sticky mass that takes time and effort to remove.

The energy of words also attaches to the room and area where we speak these words. The more time we spend in a room, the more energy builds up there. This is how psychics and empaths pick up energy from antiques and jewelry that have been in a house or worn by a person for a long time. They contain an energy imprint of that lifetime that includes the thoughts and words of the people living in these homes or wearing these items.

Now that we are aware of the creation of sticky energy that can build up in our home, imagine if you could shine a light on the walls in your home or a client's home that would reveal every word and every argument that has occurred in this home and got stuck on the walls. How does it feel?

Visualize yourself visiting a beautiful temple or church or other peaceful building, how does it feel in those rooms? What if you were in New York and could stand on the trading floor of the New York Stock Exchange? How would the energy feel in there?

When in your home or your client's home, ask yourself what kind of energy has been created there. It is possible in most cases to remove old and negative energy from a home and restore the home with new energy.

Exercise: Eight Steps to Consciously Cleansing and Psychically Changing the Energy in a Home

There are certain times of the year when a cleansing of this nature is even more powerful. The solstices and equinoxes are the most powerful times to do this type of cleansing and clearing. Psychically cleanse and recharge your home with powerful positive energy using these eight steps. These cleansing techniques are also helpful to cleanse and clear the energy when moving into a new home or after an argument or stressful situation has occurred in the home.

Step 1: Be Aware of Words in the Home

Be aware of the words you speak in your home. Your home is your temple and should be treated with love and respect. The temple of your home protects your family from the elements, provides comfort and shelter, and brings the family together to share in many activities. Consciously cleansing the home will clear the air, and using your words with conscious thought will have a positive impact on the entire family.

Step 2: Speak Kind Words

Speak loving words of encouragement, kindness, and compassion. When engaged in an argument, catch yourself. Count to ten and ask yourself what you are about to release energetically into your home and toward the people you love. Ask yourself before you speak, "Are my words kind, and are they necessary?" If they are necessary, then choose to be as kind as you can in stating them. Remain aware that what is created daily in the sacred temple of your home nurtures you and your family day and night.

Step 3: Cleanse with a Ritual

Create a cleansing ritual using white sage to smudge and purify each room. (Check with your local metaphysical store for instructions on how to properly and safely smudge with sage.)

To begin, say a prayer of protection while lighting a white candle. As you move through each room with the sage, speak a prayer or mantra to bless each room and open the windows to release the old energy outdoors.

Then sprinkle a few drops of blessed water in the corner of each room. If you are Catholic, you can ask for some holy water from your local church. You can also create blessed water yourself. Gather the purest water you can find, be it from a local spring, waterfall, or bottled artesian water. Pour the water into the container you will be using, then add a sprinkle of sea salt into the water. Place your hands over the container of water and say a prayer of your choosing that states that this water is blessed with the highest white-light energy and purity. Depending upon your religious beliefs, you can ask a particular deity to help bless this water. The intention and energy that you send is what is most important, rather than having exact words to state.

A great way to then sprinkle the blessed water in the corner of each room is to dip a sprig of fresh mint or rosemary into a small bowl of water and gently shake the sprig over the area in each corner.

If you still feel residual energy in the room, take a broom and sweep the floors. As you sweep with the broom, visualize the energy in the room being swept away and removed. Continue sweeping this energy until you reach the front door. Open the door and sweep the energy outside, visualizing it dissipating quickly into tiny droplets that soon dissolve. These particles are carried away in the wind where they break apart even further and fall to the earth.

Step 4: Paint the Walls

Paint the walls in a room in which you would like to completely change the energy. Ask for intuitive guidance to choose the color most needed in this room. Play uplifting music and as you paint, say aloud a word that you would like the room to energetically align with, such as love, peace, or grace. Lightly paint the word on the wall, while saying it aloud three times. (Be sure to quickly paint over the word before it dries, otherwise what you have written will bleed through when the paint dries.) If you are painting several rooms, create special words for each room. Abundance fits well in the dining room, peace fits in a child's room, love fits in the master bedroom, and divine order sets the intention for the entire home. If you are unable to paint your home, use a feather duster and dust the walls while focusing energy and intention on seeing the walls cleared of old energy residue.

To create a long-lasting energetic boost in your room, purchase ground quartz (sold in the paint department of home renovation stores), specially ground for paint. Hold the bag of quartz in your hands and send the desired thought into the quartz. Then mix it into the paint. This will reflect your thoughts and energy and create a beautiful sheen on the walls.

To go a step further for the ultimate in psychic protection in your home using paint, paint the ceiling of your front porch or entryway in a color called "haint blue." This light blue-green color has been used by psychics and mediums for hundreds of years and is reported to keep dark spirits away. The word "haint" is an old term meaning spirits who exist on the earth plane who do not wish anyone well by their presence. If you live in or have visited the southern part of the United States, you have most likely seen this blue-green paint on a porch or two. Many families continue the tradition without knowing the original meaning behind the color because it has always been done in their family home.

Step 5: Freshen Your Home

Add fresh flowers to bring in positive energy. Declare your home a sacred temple and keep it clutter-free. Clutter creates a detrimental effect on the energy of the room and the people who inhabit the space.

Step 6: Add Your Intention

Apply decorative lettering to the wall of any room or a piece of art that states the intention of what you wish to manifest in the home. There is a wide variety of wall decal quotes readily available in stores and online, or you can create a custom phrase of your own. With an uplifting phrase as a visual accent, it will be even easier to remember the new intentions that you are creating for your family and the sacred space you call home.

Step 7: Ring a Purifying Bell

Ring a Tibetan Buddhist bell daily to clear the energy in the home. When needed, use the dorje or striker on the bell to clear negative energy. The bell vibrates with a pure tone that radiates throughout the home, clearing negative energy and purifying the space. After ringing the bell, state your intention that the energy will now be filled in the home. Here's an example: "This home is filled with love and light. Our home is filled with peace and joy. Divine energy and love radiate through this home."

Step 8: Light a Salt Lamp

Add a Himalayan salt lamp to your home. The salt lamp exudes negative ions, which are similar to the ions created at the beach when the waves hit the shore, from a waterfall, or during a thunderstorm when lightning clears the air and moves stagnant, polluted energy. These ions generate positive energy and make you feel more relaxed and happy.

Cleansing Negative Energy from Items

Now that you've learned how to cleanse and remove negative energy from your energy bodies and from your home, you can also use this information to cleanse any item that may need it. It's fair to say, though, that some items can have such a toxic energy buildup that it is impossible to fully cleanse them, and it may be a better choice to let them go.

If you're an empath or a psychic with the ability of psychometry, you know exactly what I'm talking about here. As you further develop your psychic sensitivities, you may find that items you didn't notice energetically before now don't feel as comforting to you.

You may also find yourself wanting to redecorate and to add new inspirational items to your decor as well as finding items that you are ready to release and let go from your home. When going through these items, you may want to consider charging crystals and talismans to reflect positive energy in your home and to use with your psychic work.

Exercise: Charging Talismans and Crystals

Now that you understand the power of words as well as the energy and intention that can be emotionally released in each word, you understand the damage words can do when released in anger. You also understand the healing that words can do when released in love with a powerful healing intention.

Words are at their most powerful when used in a positive way, when they are focused on a prayer or positive affirmation that is said aloud while being expressed emotionally at the heart chakra level.

To take this positive energy activation a step further, use crystals and charge them with powerful, positive statements of energy and intention.

Gather a clear quartz crystal and place it in your right hand. In the body, the left side is the receiving side for energy, and the right side is the sending side. You are sending energy outward into the crystal, so you will want to hold it in the right hand.

Focus your thoughts and emotions on the exact intention that you want to manifest and create. Then direct that energy into the crystal as you clearly and strongly state aloud three times what you intend to create. This charges the clear quartz with energy. If it's a small crystal, you can carry the crystal with you as a touchstone (a stone that is charged and activated for a specific purpose) and reminder of what you are in the process of manifesting.

You can also use four large-sized quartz crystals and charge them with energy. The more concise, simple, and focused the manifestation, the better. Examples might include "Enhance the energy in this room so that as I sleep I am filled with healing, soothing, peaceful energy" or "Enhance the energy in my office so that creative ideas flow easily to me" or "Fill this crystal or talisman with the pure white light of protection." The crystals should only be charged with loving, positive affirmations that help create an energy field that is stimulating and conducive to positive growth. Once you have charged these crystals, place one of the four stones at each corner of the room so that they create an energy grid throughout the room, generating this energy and intention. A good stone size to use is one that fills most of the palm of your hand when you hold it.

Crystals are great to use for charging. You can also use this technique to charge a talisman or any object. Enhance that charge even more by attaching a quartz crystal to the talisman that you wish to charge with energy.

Grounding and Releasing Energy after Working in the Spirit Realms

When I was young, my mother referred to me as a "spirit walker." What she meant by this was that I had the unique ability to remain grounded on the earth plane while stepping through the veil to be in the spirit realms.

This ability is one that I've worked to develop further in this lifetime for many reasons. One of the most important is that I want to show that people with psychic ability can function very well in the physical world and have a normal life while also being psychic.

I think it's important to be in balance in this way. If you can't handle the physical world, it's difficult to be of help to others or to clearly define what you see in the spirit world.

During a recent radio interview, the host commented that he was impressed by how I have demonstrated this unique ability to remain balanced in both worlds, so much so that I teach classes on entrepreneur intuition and how to build a brand and grow your business to people with psychic ability. I love teaching how to be balanced in both realms so that psychics can build their businesses and live the life of their dreams, doing what they love to do using their psychic abilities.

This is no different from anyone else with a special talent. Everyone has to learn how to balance their energy so that they can achieve their personal best. All artistic and creative types go through this process when they find the way to tune in to their creative side and let the art come out but then aren't sure what to do next to get the art to the people to enjoy it.

To succeed, they must find a way to ground their energy when they are done with the creative project so that they can also function well in the logical, earthly world.

Those who haven't been trained to ground back into the physical plane after visiting the spiritual planes are often left to their own devices. That can lead to some unhealthy practices as they struggle to find a way to feel connected back to the earth plane again. The following are some examples of how to ground your energy.

Stand Barefoot on the Grass

The chakras in the soles of your feet will immediately reach out to the earth and root you back to the earth plane. Walking in sand will do this as well, and if you need to remove some sticky energy, sand is a great absorber of energy.

If stuck indoors, remove your shoes and wiggle your toes.

Then stand up and raise your arms in the air. Instead of reaching up to pull in more energy, gently lower your arms, breathe deeply, and lower the energy around you, closing the field. Then cross your arms over your chest, making the shape of an X in order to seal the energy in.

Have a Quick Bite to Eat

The act of mindful eating brings you back into your body as you focus on chewing the food. The digestion in the stomach also grounds you back into your body through this process. Fruits and chocolate are very helpful to grounding. It's different for each person. I know some psychics who eat the biggest steak they can find in order to ground themselves back into their bodies after a big day of doing readings.

Hold a Touchstone

Crystals are very powerful tools for connecting with the other side. Some crystals, though, can help us tap back into our physical selves and bring us back to center. You can program a quartz crystal to do this act when you hold it in your hand, or you may be drawn to a specific type of crystal or gemstone that you activate to do this work. A stone that has been charged or activated for a specific purpose like this is called a "touchstone."

Even a stone (nongemstone) that fits nicely in the palm of your hand can be charged into a touchstone that grounds you and brings you back to yourself. Gemstones are the most popular, though. The ones that are most frequently used include black tourmaline, hematite, and amethyst.

Take a Shower or a Sea-Salt Bath

Standing in the water connects you back to the physical plane and removes any residue that may have gathered around you. If you've been doing psychic work and need help to remove energy residue from another person, taking a bath with some sea salt will cleanse your aura and ground you. You can also take a shower, use a salt scrub, and visualize the energy residue floating away down the drain.

Close the Energy Loop

Did you always wonder why it felt like your mother had eyes in the back of her head? It's because she did, and so do you. The occipital nerves are located in the back of your skull near the neck, and this is a highly sensitive area where we sense things psychically. Place your hand over the back of your head over this area to stop energy from flowing in and then take your other hand and cover it over your third eye chakra area to stop energy from flowing out and upward.

Keep your hands over these two areas for thirty seconds. This will close the energy flow, allowing you to reset your energy and ground your body without the outside influences and energy swirling around you.

Nine

GHOSTS AND SPIRITS

Now that you've learned how to ground yourself and you've identified and worked with some of the exercises to open up psychically, you may be having experiences such as flashes of intuition, dreams that are coming true, and possibly even visits from a being from the spiritual planes. What are the different types of beings, and what do they want with you when they visit? Our journey continues as we explore ghosts and spirits. Let's take a peek.

I've had many experiences with the supernatural and paranormal realms. In my work, I share my experience and training in workshops around the country. I teach others how to become more intuitive, how to connect with the other side, how to sense negative energy in a home or building, and, more importantly, how to discern whether the energy can be removed and cleansed or whether it is best left alone.

I've observed a rise in paranormal activity that corresponds to the lifting of the veil between the earth plane and the spiritual realms at this time. I believe that a conscious evolution is occurring on the mind, body, and spirit level, and as this evolution continues, many people will connect with their intuitive abilities and be able to communicate with the spirit world, including with ghosts that have remained on the earth plane.

Seeing Ghosts

As a psychic and paranormal researcher, many people have asked me what it's like to see or sense a ghost. The best way I can describe the experience is that most of the ghostly activity that I feel immediately when entering a new space or building is the haunting activity of a time loop, or energy-imprint recording.

These types of hauntings are not examples of interacting with active ghosts. They represent a moment in time that has become burned into the energy field of a thing or place. I describe this "time-loop haunting" as energy that was traumatic and so strong that it created an energy imprint that attached itself to this area, whether it be a piece of land, a home, or even a car. There is not an active ghost there at the location—at least, not often. Instead, the traumatic experience created such a powerful imprint that it can be viewed and felt by someone who is psychically sensitive.

This type of paranormal haunting is the easiest to detect anytime because, for me, it's like watching a projector playing a movie. To imagine what this looks like to me, picture walking into a home that you've never been in before. You don't know your way around, so you cautiously enter the home. You've been told that no one is home, but as you continue walking through the rooms, you hear a sound. As your ears strain to detect where the sound is coming from, you hear the soft murmur and whisper of voices. You are now fairly sure that someone is here in the house, but you are not sure in what room.

You're a little ill at ease because you've been told the house is empty, but you can hear the sound of voices. As you move toward them, they are getting stronger and louder. There is a closed door, and you can see a bit of light coming from this room and softly open the door to see what's inside.

As the door opens, you see what looks like an image from a projector that has been left on, playing a family movie. The projected image plays a scene from the family's life, and when it ends, it rewinds and plays the movie over and over again. Sometimes the image is crystal clear, and sometimes it's worn and old, with parts of the film missing, having burned away like the old celluloid films that would become damaged on the reel in old theaters. Many times, this is similar to what I see, only there's no projector rolling. The scene is just happening in the room, like a 3-D movie being projected in the open.

These energy imprints, or time loops, are one type of haunting. The time loop runs on a frequent basis like a movie, appearing nightly at a haunted house near you.

Ghosts in the time loop are not truly ghosts, in the sense that no part of the soul is still here on the earth plane. Rather, this is an energy imprint playing in an area blasted with strong emotional and psychic residue from a traumatic experience. A good example of this type of haunting is the battlefield in Gettysburg, Pennsylvania, where so many men died quickly and horrifically during the Civil War. It left a strong, negative energetic impact that can be felt and seen by many people who visit the battlefield each year. There are hundreds of reports by people who have witnessed these ghostly soldiers repeat the battle scene on moonlit nights.

Ghostly visitations and apparitions that I have experienced, on the other hand, are much more subjective. The ghost has the free will to appear or not appear and decides whether or not to engage you.

This is why on ghost television shows and investigations you will see some investigators attempting to draw out the ghosts to interact with them by asking them rude questions, yelling at them, or goading them at times to make them angry enough to show themselves.

I don't recommend doing this, as you may run into the wrong ghost who may decide that they are now angry enough to spend their time hanging around you, rather than hanging around where they have been.

One thing ghosts have that we don't is all the free time in the world. They don't eat, they don't sleep, and they don't need to work for a living. Would you really want to antagonize a being like this who has all the time they want to mess with you? Or worse, what if it's not a ghost but an entity that is stronger and could cause even more trouble for you?

Most of us don't go to a dangerous part of town and attempt to pick a fight with thugs, inviting them to show us what they've got, so why would we want to invite this kind of trouble with a ghost? Most of the people that I've met who do this quickly regret their actions.

My advice is to tread lightly and respectfully when ghost hunting. Have respect for the living and the dead at each location. Protect yourself at all times and ask politely to connect with the other side, in the same manner you would if you were knocking on a stranger's door and asking to tour their home.

The simplest way to define the difference between a ghost and a spirit is that ghosts remain bound to the earth plane. They do not cross over to the higher planes. For whatever reason, at their moment of death as a human, they decide to remain in their spirit form on the earth plane.

Because of this decision, they do not cross over to the spirit world and reunite with their higher-soul self. Instead, they remain a pale shadow of themselves, connected only to their personality and the appearance of the lifetime they just left.

As I explain to my students, when we die, there are three cords attached inside of us that wrap up all the energy and essence of our being.

These cords take all of our thoughts, emotions, and personality back up into the spiritual planes, where they are stored in the akashic records and easily accessed to review on the other side.

If for some reason the person who dies does not go into the light, a part of their spirit remains here on earth. The cords still detach from the body, bringing the information and essence of the person back up into their akashic records, but it is incomplete because part of the soul of the person is still here on the earth plane.

The reasons some people stay behind as ghosts are varied. Some people fear what they've been told awaits them on the other side—judgment, retribution, punishment, or, according to some spiritual beliefs, a terrible place called hell. If people fear that they have done a terrible wrong, they may be too frightened to cross over and meet their fate, so they remain here on the earth plane in limbo.

Other ghosts stay for a specific purpose. They don't want to separate from their families, loved ones, or a career or lifestyle that they love. They want to be around to see what happens in these scenarios and aren't ready to let it go. They don't realize that they can cross over into the higher planes and in their spirit form still view what is going on here on earth.

Some ghosts die a traumatic death and are unaware that they have died. They were killed instantly in a battle or an accident and became stuck here in limbo since they don't truly understand what has happened to them.

We've all heard the stories of the girl in the prom dress walking down the road at night. A car pulls over to drive her into town, and she talks to the driver along the way, only to disappear from the seat at a certain mile marker on the road. Her ghost is attached to the place on the road where she died in a car accident. At certain times of the year, near the anniversary of her death or under certain conditions, her ghost appears walking down the road, still trying to get to the prom that she was so excited about attending that evening.

These types of ghosts have a hard time accepting the reality that their death was twenty or forty years ago and can prove to be the most difficult to help.

The ghosts who have consciously stayed behind on the earth plane in an attempt to remain close to their family or out of fear of retribution on the other side are easier to work with. A psychic medium can help them understand the situation and how they can proceed to the spirit world where all will be fine.

The Higher Self and Human Spirits

Spirits are beings who have crossed over to the other side and come back at will to visit the earth plane. When the human body dies, the soul is released, and it travels back with the three energy cords as they detach from the aura and chakras. The soul reunites with the higher self, or whole soul, on the higher spiritual realms.

At this point, the soul can occasionally return to visit on the earth plane, appearing in what we call "spirit form." In spirit form, the soul appears as it was known in its most recent lifetime, but it can also choose to appear as it looked in previous lifetimes.

The question I am most often asked about the soul, reincarnation, and how spirits can continue to visit is this: "If it is true that a person reincarnates back on to earth every seven to ten years, then how is it that my mother still appears to me in spirit form and visits me? She has been dead for twenty years and must have already reincarnated back here to earth in a new body." The answer has to do with the higher self of each person, where the full embodiment of the soul of each person resides.

Think of the shape of the soul in the higher spirit planes as an upside-down pyramid. The base of the pyramid is the largest section, which is where all of our soul resides. It contains our entire essence and all of our memories from each lifetime.

When we reincarnate back on earth, only a small part of our soul drops down from this upside-down pyramid into our earthly body. It drops down through the bottom tip of the pyramid, like a tiny bit of frosting being squeezed out of a tube.

The cords from our higher self stay attached to this part of our soul as the part anchors into the human body. These cords relay all of our experiences back and forth from our human form to our higher self, or soul body.

Therefore, only a small part of the soul is located in the physical body. This part is only aware of a small part of who we are, and it remains focused on the purpose and destiny for our incarnation in this particular lifetime. Reports of how we are doing and making progress on these endeavors are sent back through the cords and up to the higher self, where the majority of the soul always resides.

Because the higher self, or soul body, contains all of our lifetimes and information and is not contained in a small, human body, it can multitask. So when the higher self receives a "call" from someone on the earth plane asking to speak with a part of that soul that was formerly known as a parent, sibling, or spouse, it can recall that specific lifetime and memory and send a soul expression in that form from that lifetime down to communicate with the soul on earth who is asking to speak with them.

When this particular aspect of the soul comes to the earth plane to communicate, they may or may not be much wiser on the subject that we desire to speak with them about. It depends on how old or young this soul is in regard to how many lifetimes of experiences they have had, what they have learned, and what they have avoided learning.

Just because someone has passed over to the other side does not mean that they are endowed with great knowledge. The spirit plane has many levels, and the soul only proceeds to the highest level that it is allowed entrance into, based upon the karma and experiences of the soul.

This is a deep, esoteric teaching that I can only briefly discuss in this book, but it is one that I teach in depth to my students who study with me at my school, the Academy of Mystical Arts and Spiritual Sciences.

The previous example describes spirit visitations from people who were humans in a past life. There are also visitations from spirit guides, angels and other nonhuman entities. The more you open to your psychic abilities and awaken this part of yourself, the more opportunities to interact with other beings of light will come.

Exercise: Inviting Loved Ones in Spirit to Visit with You

There are certain pockets of time each year when the portals to the spirit world are easier to pass through, both for spirits to visit the earth plane and for those of us here on earth to visit the other planes. The three days around Halloween (October 30 through November 1) are one of these times when the veil is easily pierced.

During this three-day period, many people choose to connect with their loved ones on the other side. One of the ways to reach out and connect with your loved ones in spirit is to host what is called a "dumb supper." The word "dumb" in this context refers to its earlier meaning of "silent" or "mute." Silence is observed during this dinner so that people may sit quietly and reflect and honor those who have gone on to the other side. It also allows for information to come through from the spirit world.

To create this ritual in your home, prepare a dinner to serve in a formal fashion to your guests in attendance. Set a place setting at the table for the loved one you would like to invite to attend the dinner from the spirit world. At this place setting, leave the chair empty and place a photograph of the person next to the place setting. Also place a personal item of theirs, such as a watch or other piece of jewelry, at this setting. Put food on the plate and fill the wine glass so that the visiting spirit may partake of the essence of the food through the spirit realms.

Psychic self-defense and protective measures must first be assured in order to safely take this journey, so, as always when engaging in work with the spirit world, put a force field of pure white light around you. Visualize your body being surrounded by a bubble of pure white light. Then, speaking aloud, ask to be surrounded by the pure white light, while visualizing this light surrounding your body. State aloud that only good comes to you, only good comes from you, and only that which is for your highest and best good can be made to manifest to you. You can add your own personalized sayings to this as you create the white-light force field, asking that the room be filled with the pure white light, that each person in the room is protected and surrounded in this field of pure white light, and that the only spirits who are allowed to visit are the ones that the group specifically names aloud during the event.

Typically the room is softly lit by candlelight, and a period of silence is observed in which there is no talking at the beginning of the event. During this period of silence, ask each person to focus on the person that the group has chosen to invite to visit from the spirit world. The host surrounds the room in a protective white-light circle of energy and asks the spirits from the highest realms to guard and protect the circle and the people at the table. Then the host invites guests to speak and share fond memories of the spirit, who is the guest of honor, in order to share how loved the spirit is and how the spirit's memory remains strong with their family and friends on earth. The host should speak this invitation aloud, asking the person in the spirit world to come and visit with family and friends if they are able to do so this evening.

After the event is over, cross your arms over your chest in an X formation and ask everyone else to do the same. Thank the spirits for visiting and announce aloud that the connection between this world and the spirit world is now closed. Visualize the energetic and psychic connection dissipating and dissolving, and see the veil closed. Then extinguish any candles that you have lit and open a window if possible to clear the room.

Exercise: Private Ritual to See Ancestors When the Veil is Thin

Create an altar to connect with your loved one in spirit. On a table, place a photograph of and a personal item once owned by the person in the spirit world whom you are attempting to reach.

Light a white candle, draw a circle of protective white light around you, and then ask to communicate with the person in spirit. Speak of the person in detail, calling them by name and mentioning a fond memory that will connect them to you. Here's an example: "Hello, Aunt Rose. I remember how I loved to be in your kitchen when we would make pies together at the holidays."

Explain situations and memories like this so that they are drawn back to that particular lifetime with you. Remember, they have had lots of lifetimes and continue forward into new ones, so you want to help them connect to you as the person they were when you knew them. The average cycle of turn-around time for a spirit to reincarnate on the earth plane is between three and ten years, and seven is the average. The time differs according to what the soul is doing on the other side. If you are attempting to reach out to a grandparent who passed away twenty years ago, for example, chances are that they rein-carnated back to this earth plane at least ten years ago and are living a new life as a child on earth, possibly as a new member of your family. You can still connect with the energy of your grandparent's soul, as each person's higher self remains intact in the part of their soul that remains on the spiritual planes. Only a small portion of the soul is inside of the physical body here on earth. The higher-self part of your soul retains all memories and information from all of its lifetimes, so it can connect with you and reach out to communicate regarding the lifetime that you are speaking about.

In order to connect with the person you are trying to reach, you will need to reach out to their higher self and remind them which life incarnation you remember them from. The easiest way to do this is to prompt memories of your specific lifetime with your loved one. If they are recently deceased, it is easier to connect with this most-recent lifetime, but if it's an ancient ancestor, you will have to do things to trigger them to connect with this part of their soul and their akashic records in order to recall that lifetime. This is why a personal article of theirs that they can energetically connect with is very helpful. A photograph is also useful because it sends the mental image and memory imprint of the person they were when they incarnated into this particular lifetime.

When they arrive from the spirit realm, have a notebook nearby so you can jot down notes of things you receive intuitively during this time. You may also want to use a digital recorder during this event to see if you can record an electronic voice phenomenon (EVP). An EVP is a recording of a voice or sound from a spirit that you could not physically hear during its emission. The person in spirit form may not be able to communicate directly with their voice at all. Instead you may see images that come to you psychically through your third eye, as it is easier for them to communicate telepathically in this manner.

In most spirit communications of this type, the spirit either appears quickly or doesn't appear at all. The visits are brief, usually around five minutes and typically not lasting longer than fifteen minutes. Once you have completed the session with spirit, thank them for coming. Then cross your arms over your chest in an X formation and ask everyone else to do the same. Announce aloud that the connection between this world and the spirit world is now closed. Visualize the energetic and psychic connection dissipating and dissolving, and see the veil closed. Then extinguish any candles that you have lit and open a window if possible to clear the room.

Ghost or Spirit Energy Sources

When you encounter a ghost, you generally were not actively seeking the experience. Rather, you "happened upon" the ghost when you arrived at a location. Ghosts typically are attached to buildings or locations that they frequented when they were alive.

Communication may be possible if the ghost is one of the types that is aware of having passed and opted to stay here on the earth plane. Some ghosts may not communicate except to ask for a ride, like the ghost girl going to prom, while others in an energy imprint do not engage you at all. It's not good to interact with ghosts for any length of time regardless of their type, as they are shadow selves, not fully realized, and they are stuck here on the earth plane.

Because of this, they are not filled with the light from the spirit planes, which renews their energy. Instead, they must pull on energy from other sources in order to interact and to materialize. This is why lights blink off and on, batteries die, and electronics go haywire when there is a ghost around—ghosts are pulling from any source of energy that they can to get enough energy to materialize and communicate.

They can also pull energy from humans, which you want to avoid, as it drains your vital, restorative resources and aura energy. I've often seen this in paranormal researchers who spend too much time ghost hunting.

They began to get a sallow look about them, with dark circles under their eyes, and their aura becomes greatly diminished in shape and light. Their interactions with the paranormal entities exact a toll on them as the ghosts pull from their vital energy.

Spirits, on the other hand, often appear with a glow of light around them, sourcing their own energy from the higher planes. They are able to use this energy source to manifest. The higher the plane the spirits come from, the more light you'll see around them, and they will never ask to use you or your body in any way.

Lower-level spirits, who reside on the lower astral planes, are the ones who haven't been able to graduate into the higher planes. These are the ones who will attempt to communicate with a person by asking to take over their body. They don't have the power to materialize using their own resources, so they have to pull energy from the human. It is never a good idea to allow lower-level spirits to inhabit your body or home because they will quickly drain your energy and vitality. They may choose not to leave when you want them to, and when you try to make them leave, you may find that you don't have the strength to do so. For that reason, you don't want to invite these spirits into your home or into your body.

In my experience, I have found that spirits of the highest energy have a variety of powerful ways to appear and communicate directly with me. They do not require the use of my body in order to do so. The stories of things going wrong for a person during a spirit visitation usually begin when they invite one of these lower-astral-plane spirits to be around them and to come into their body. I advise against allowing any spirit to do this to you and your body. Also ask them why, if they claim to be advanced higher-level spirits, they would need to do so.

Working with Spirit Guides

In chapter 4, I shared an exercise in which you invite your spirit guide to work with you during meditation. I also mentioned inviting your spirit guides to join you when you are traveling to the other side to work, including for protection when visiting the akashic records.

Our spirit guides are always with us and are ready to help in any capacity that they can. They cannot do the work for us and most times they cannot directly interfere with anything we are doing. What they can do is offer hints and suggestions and when we ask them directly, they can help show the right path to follow. The most important thing to remember is that you have to ask them directly for their assistance. They cannot offer it otherwise.

Ten

ETHICS, PROTOCOL, AND RESPONSIBILITIES WITH READINGS

I teach people around the world how to tap into their psychic abilities, and I always begin with this tip: Listen to your intuition, trust in the process, and have the courage and fortitude to find the reading style that is right for you.

Create a list of guidelines based on the wisdom of your experience from your readings, and write your own psychic handbook in this way. My handbook is focused on always asking for the highest and best guidance from the other side when delivering information, so that it is only helpful and never hurtful for the person I am sharing information with.

The guidelines I put into place are the reason my psychic work has flourished over the years. It is greatly based on creating trust and building a strong connection with my clients. They trust that I am honest and direct with them. If they book me for a consultation and I need to tell them something difficult, they trust that I will deliver this information to them as compassionately as possible. They know that when I share this knowledge, I will also provide helpful tips on how they can take this challenging information and turn it into an opportunity to grow.

I've also shared that there are times when I don't feel that I can offer the best service to a client, and when a time like this occurs, I recommend them to another professional who I think can best meet their needs.

This creates a strong relationship built on trust and respect. In this line of work, it is integral that we build this strong foundation, as we all work to bring a sense of professionalism, decorum, and legitimacy to the work that we do in this field.

It's also important to protect yourself by setting boundaries, which you will do when you create a list of rules and guidelines that you follow as a psychic. Many psychics follow protocols similar to those used by therapists. They don't get too personally involved with their clients on an emotional, personal, or relationship level. They also set firm boundaries for the amount of time that they will read and are not available at all times.

You are sharing information with people that can have a life-altering effect upon them. Always remember this so that you never flippantly share information in a casual or callous way. This work is meant to be shared with the highest amount of respect and with the understanding that you are sharing information that can have a long-term effect on the person at the mind, body, and spirit level.

Personal Ethics

There are also personal ethical questions that you should ask yourself regarding your psychic ability. Here are some examples:

Should I share the information that I am seeing with this person?

You are stepping into a new realm of responsibility as a person with psychic ability. The information that you see can potentially negatively affect a person's life. Many people look for a psychic reading when they are at low points in their lives and things are not going well, so it's very important to be gentle and kind when relaying information in these types of readings. This requires careful consideration before just blurting out information to them, as it could have a profound effect on them for the rest of their lives.

I remember chatting with a person who had only had one psychic reading in their life in their early twenties. This psychic had told them that something terrible would happen to them if they got married, so they had been avoiding getting into a serious relationship for years. When I asked them more about the reading, I was able to show them that this prediction was not the case. The psychic had been referring only to the person they had been dating at the time of the reading, not about dating anyone anytime in the future.

When sharing psychic information with people, make sure you are very clear about what it is that you are seeing and, if possible, explain the timelines and how changing your thoughts can change the future. It's also very important to explain that nothing that you see is carved in stone as the exact future. Always explain that each person has free will and that free will is the strongest energy out there. No matter what potential outcome you are seeing psychically, explain that free will is always stronger and can change the outcome.

Is the information that this person is asking me about for the highest and best good?

A person may ask you for a reading that is actually all about another person in their life. Maybe they are attracted to a person who is in a relationship, and they want to know if this person will leave their partner and be with them. They are in essence asking you to read the thoughts and intentions of this other person. You will need to decide what your code of ethics is in sharing information of this kind. Most psychics won't read the thoughts of the other person: this creates karma for them, and nothing is worth that price. It's one thing to read for a person who asks you to do so, but it's something completely different to pry into another person's energy fields without their permission.

When asked this question in a reading, the psychic will usually tap into the energy fields of the person asking the question to see if the other person's energy has been engaging with the client's for a long period of time. If the psychic sees that the energy is not very strong and intermingled with this person, that gives clues that a strong relationship is not building between the two people. This way, the psychic has not pried into the other person's life and is just reading which people are invested energetically and long term with the person asking the question.

Are there questions that I shouldn't answer ever?

As you develop your abilities and grow stronger with them, you will see more and more about each person you connect with on a psychic level. You'll receive a wide range of questions and some may surprise you. Some people will ask you if you see the date of their death. Most psychics will not give this information to a person for a variety of reasons, one of the biggest being that predicting time is very, very difficult to do. What is seen timewise in the spirit world does not accurately translate to earth-plane time. Almost every psychic will tell you this. Time is the most difficult thing to predict with any sense of accuracy. Most psychics get a sense of timelines, such as if something is coming soon, in the next six months, or in the next two years, or that it's further away or will happen later in life. For this reason and for other moral and ethical reasons, most psychics will not share information regarding such a deeply personal question as time of death.

Another question to avoid answering is one related to a person's health. You are not a medical professional and should never give medical advice. If you see something that looks out of order with the person's physical health, suggest getting a full checkup by a doctor. Anything else that you might say could affect their thoughts and beliefs about their health, which could be scary and greatly affect them in a negative way.

Do I want to be a psychic reader?

At first, it's best to work on just honing your abilities to discover what you are comfortable with doing and what you enjoy. Opening up to your psychic abilities is a bit like opening Pandora's box. Once it's been opened, it never fully closes again. If you decide that you don't like knowing things psychically, you can block it out for the most part and not have feelings that are as strong, but you'll still be in touch with your intuition. If you decide that you like exploring your psychic side, you may decide one day to take it a step further and turn it into a career. There are many different career paths in which you can incorporate your psychic ability beyond what you may imagine of just reading for people. People use their psychic abilities in the financial world, in real estate, to build their chosen career, as entrepreneurs building their business, in therapy and life coaching, in healing modalities, and in teaching. Being in tune with your psychic ability just provides more creative options in your life along with a deeper understanding into seeing how the world works.

Eleven

STANDARDS AND CHALLENGES
OF BEING PSYCHIC

One of the toughest challenges of reading for people as a psychic is that you are held to impossible standards. Sometimes these are unbelievably impossible standards that no one else in the world is held to for their abilities.

People expect psychics to be 100 percent accurate, 100 percent of the time. This is impossible. "Then you are not psychic," you say. "If you don't know everything, then you are not psychic."

This is simply not true, and, like with every other ability, no one is perfect. Psychic ability is a skill and an art, not a perfect science. When you are reading the energy swirling around a person, you are seeing all of their thoughts, desires, emotions, wishes, and karmic influences. All of these things are fluid and interchanging moment by moment. Many times what you are seeing are the thoughts that the person has been focused on for a long time or the emotions that are the strongest emitting from their energy fields. For example, if someone has been in love with a partner for a long time and wants to be with them, even when the partner is not treating them well, you will see their desire to be with this partner. As you tap into the energy field of the partner, you will see their energy field and their thoughts of betraying the other person and possibly looking to end the relationship.

Our thoughts and emotions are expressed in these energy fields, and what we focus on the most is the direction we are heading and the path we are heading toward. When you read a person's energy field, you will see the path they are on due to where they are putting their energy. You'll also see karmic markers that help attract certain people and situations to them for experiences they need to have in this lifetime. You might read for this person a year later and see a completely new path in front of them if something has drastically changed in their life and they have aligned their thoughts and emotions in a new direction. For example, maybe out of the blue the person finally grew tired of the relationship in which they were not being treated well, so they took the initiative and got a divorce. That is a free-will action that they took on their own, and when they did, they changed the path they were on energetically. Now when you read for them a year later, their free-will decision has opened a variety of new paths before them. Their thoughts and emotional energy have shifted and are now exuding new energy that can attract new people and situations into their lives.

If there was a karmic marker in their aura that attracted the last relationship to their life, such as a lesson to be learned about not losing balance in a relationship, you can check to see if this marker is still there or if it has dissolved. If it's still there, you can remind them of this so that they think about how they lost themselves in the last relationship and how to find balance within themselves first, to avoid repeating this experience in the new relationship. If the marker is gone, congratulate them on having learned what they needed to learn from the previous relationship, and explain how to fill this space in the aura with positive energy and new thoughts of what they would like to experience in their new relationship. This is one of thousands of examples of how you can help someone when reading for them.

Like I said earlier, though, it's not a perfect science. When you read someone, you are seeing the fields around them and what they are in the process of manifesting through their wants, desires, thoughts, emotions, destiny, and karmic markers. Happily, because of free will, their paths can change at any time. This is great and also challenging, as it means that the data you can see is changing constantly for each person.

When you are reading for a person and you move beyond their energy fields and are looking into the spiritual planes for information to help them, this information is often presented to you in images and brief bits of data that come through quickly. I've mentioned that for me it's like seeing a short movie clip about the person. I don't get the whole movie, just a minute or so, and then I have to discern what this short movie is trying to explain to me. Some of these are more straightforward than others, and over time you'll get better and better at reading what they mean. Additionally, the spirit world moves in its own direction and sense of time, which is very different from the earth plane. Some visits over there are clearer than others, and many parts of it are still a mystery to us. So when you gather information from the other side, it's never quite the same.

As we better understand psychic abilities and more people share what they experience, it will help everyone understand how this process works. Right now, because many people do not understand psychic ability, their litmus test for true psychic ability is knowing everything about everything and everyone in the world, and the readings must be repeatable constantly with no room for error. Psychic or not, we are still human, and as humans we are not perfect. No one can be held to this level of perfection.

For example, in baseball, the best batter in the world does not step up to the plate and hit a home run every single time. That is the equivalent of the standard that a psychic is held up to with a reading.

In the medical field, doctors do not save every patient, nor do they diagnose every patient's illness correctly every single time. Life and people are complicated. A psychic, like a doctor, sees clues and hints to what is going on with the person and does their best to help in any way possible.

As a person with intuitive ability, the more you work to hone your skills, the better psychic you will become. You learn how to connect with your higher self, with the other side, and with your guides. You find better ways to quiet your mind and open your energy in a clear way. Like any other ability, practice doesn't really make perfect, but it brings us as close as can be achieved according to our talent and drive in our field. So keep in mind that this is your personal journey and that developing psychic ability is an art more than a science. This means that each person finds and develops their unique style that works best for them. While I can offer guidelines and tips and techniques to try out, as you continue to practice, you'll find the ways that work best for you. Trust your intuition and let your higher self be your guide, as there is no better instructor for you than your higher self, who knows you better than anyone!

Keep a Notebook and Make Observations

One of the best practices that helped me understand what I was seeing as I was developing my abilities as a psychic was to keep notes on what I was seeing around each person.

When I was young, I saw the aura around each person and found it fascinating. I loved watching the colors, the shapes, and how the aura changed around each person as they said and did different things.

I observed how a person's aura would be open and relaxed and flowing. As someone came into the room that they did not like, I saw how their aura would pull in around them. It would tighten up and get thick, creating an energy shield around the person.

This person would unconsciously be creating this blockage of energy to literally push the other person away. They were building a wall so that the other person's energy, comments, and actions would not penetrate them as deeply as they could have if the person's aura had continued to be open and flowing in a receptive mode.

I would watch another person in a conversation who was unaware of the angry energy pent up in the aura of the person they were speaking with. They did not yet know that angry energy would soon be coming at them from this other person. They would be caught off guard in a conversation that was flowing nicely, and then out of the blue the other person would say something rude and hurtful. I could see how these words wrapped up in the angry energy bubble emitted outward from their body. This bubble would strike the other person and cause great ripples in their aura, like being hit with poison arrows.

Fascinated by these interactions, I began to keep notes on what I saw and how it altered each person's aura and emotional field. I also kept notes on things I would see appearing in the aura, including shapes, symbols, and diffused colors. As I spent more time around a person, I saw how these shapes eventually manifested in the person's life. Sometimes the shapes appeared as a physical manifestation; at other times they would manifest in a mental or emotional capacity.

The more I observed and studied what I was seeing, the better I became at reading auras and understanding what each color, shape, and symbol meant.

Take notes. The same work applies in all types of psychic work. The more people you read for, the more experience you'll gain reading their energy fields from the physical, mental, emotional, and spiritual layers.

You'll find over time that when a certain image, like a pink rose, appears to you during readings, the color and the size and texture of the image will have a specific meaning that applies to whomever it is shone to during a reading. For example, the pink color of the rose will have a specific meaning over red, yellow, or white, and even the state of the rose will give hints to the meaning.

Is it a rosebud, fully closed and yet to have opened? A closed bud means they are holding on to things too tightly and so there is no room for new growth or energy to come in. Or is it a rose in full bloom? A rose in full bloom means the person should be congratulated on accomplishing something that they have done very well.

Both types hold clues to what spirit is trying to tell you in regard to how the person is doing and feeling.

The more you work with your intuition and connect with the higher planes and your guides, the easier these symbols become to interpret, for you will have observed and recognized them through many readings.

Challenges of Being Psychic

As a psychic, sometimes you'll see the future even when you're not expecting to do so. You may have experienced this if you are naturally intuitive; out of the blue you might have a vision of something that comes to pass or a vivid dream that later becomes reality.

I've had dreams and visions like that my whole life. Some of them are very clear and easy to understand, while others take some work to interpret. I've had to access my research with dream interpretation symbols and other information to discern what the dream was trying to tell me.

Sometimes the information that you receive is unpleasant or uncomfortable to see. It can be about a person that you know, or you may see something about an event coming up in the future that you can do little to stop, like an earth change or major storm that will affect a large area of the world. It's important to understand the scope and variety of things you will see as a psychic along with the realization that there are things beyond your control that will occur in the world.

Another side effect to being psychic that surprises many people when they awaken their abilities is that once they are able to tell others something about their lives that the psychic had no other way of knowing, this changes the way those people feel about the psychic.

Some people are excited by this news and want the psychic to constantly tell them everything about their life. This is not a good thing to agree to, as the person can become overly dependent on this information, wanting readings way too often in order to make every decision in their lives. As a psychic, you'll need to decide how often you will do a reading for someone so that it doesn't become a crutch in their life.

On the flip side, as you begin to share your psychic abilities, whether you do readings as part of your work or just share with others what you feel psychically, some people will be scared by this revelation. They may have reactions that truly surprise you, such as wanting to avoid you because they think you are scanning them and reading their thoughts all of the time or because of their religious beliefs, which conflict with the concept of this being a natural ability. Due to their religious beliefs, some people believe that psychic ability is a negative ability caused by evil spirits. You may find that some people will pull away from you when they see that you have psychic ability.

Other times, people reject the existence of your abilities entirely. I've spent a good amount of time in this lifetime engaging with scientists and researchers explaining the metaphysical types of energy relationships. When they say they cannot find definitive proof with their eyes, I patiently remind them that absence of evidence by their protocol and eyes is not proof of absence. I ask how many of them are color blind and without fail, a few of them will raise their hands. I then explain, "If we were going by your 'evidence' as a color blind person and what you can see, the rest of us would be deemed crazy or liars if we claim to see the color red. Just because your eyes aren't attuned to see what others can see, that does not mean that it does not exist." I can only hope this gives them some further thought to consider infinite possibilities.

These are all situations that you'll need to consider when opening up to your psychic abilities. With any new change that you make, there is always a response from other people in your life. Change of any kind can make some people very uncomfortable. Over time, those who stick around will see that you are still the person they know. All that's changed is that you developed some new tools to tap into your intuition to help yourself and, in many cases, others.

CONCLUSION

The true gift of psychic ability is to help people see where destiny and free will are taking them on their soul path in this lifetime. It allows them to consider the future in a variety of paths and directions and to choose which direction may be the best one for them to take.

Psychic abilities can help each of us see who we are, why we are here, how to be our best in relationships, and how to reach our personal highest and best life. Despite a few challenges, it is very fulfilling to be able to tap into this information and help yourself and others when possible.

Over the years as you continue to hone your psychic abilities, you may find that what you understand about yourself may change. The experiences you will have working in the psychic field and in the spirit world may open you up to exploring deeper esoteric concepts and set you on a path of new metaphysical and spiritual exploration. My teacher used to call this peeling back the onion, explaining that there are many layers to be revealed before you reach the core. I've always found this exciting—that there is more to be revealed and explored, both while we are here on earth in this physical body experience and on the other side when we return.

I hope by the time you've reached this point in the book that we've connected and bonded a little along the way. I've shared some of my experiences as a psychic and how this journey has evolved for me over this lifetime in the hopes that they will help you along your path.

My wish for you, my dear psychic friend, is this: May these teachings and psychic tools bless you and serve you well, not just as you read this book but for the years to come as you continue your journey of soul exploration on this earth.

In love, light, and a grand sense of adventure!

BIBLIOGRAPHY

Ambrose, Kala. *The Awakened Aura: Experiencing the Evolution of Your Energy Body*. Woodbury, MN: Llewellyn Publications, 2011.

———. *9 Life Altering Lessons: Secrets of the Mystery Schools Unveiled*. Los Angeles: Reality Press, 2007.

———. *Spirits of New Orleans: Voodoo Curses, Vampire Legends, and Cities of the Dead*. Covington, KY: Clerisy Press, 2011.

Andrews, Ted. *How to See and Read the Aura*. Woodbury, MN: Llewellyn Publications, 2008.

Bailey, Alice. *Esoteric Healing: A Treatise on the Seven Rays*. London: Lucis Publishing, 1972.

Besant, Annie, and C. W. Leadbeater. *Thought-Forms*. New York: Quest Books, 1999.

Blavatsky, H. P. *Isis Unveiled: Secrets of the Ancient Wisdom Tradition, Madame Blavatsky's First Work*. Abr. Ed. Wheaton, IL: Quest Books, 1997.

———. *The Secret Doctrine*. New York: Tarcher, 2009.

Butler, W. E. *How to Read the Aura and Practice Psychometry, Telepathy and Clairvoyance*. New York: Destiny Books, 1998.

Campbell, Joseph. *The Power of Myth*. New York: Random House, 2011.

Cayce, Edgar. *Reincarnation and Karma*. Virginia Beach, VA: A.R.E. Press, 2005.

Fortune, Dion. *Psychic Self-Defense: The Classic Instruction Manual for Protecting Yourself Against Paranormal Attack*. Newburyport, MA: Weiser, 2011.

Hall, Manly P. *The Secret Teachings of All Ages*. New York: Tarcher, 2003.

Hay, Louise. *Heal Your Body*. Carlsbad, CA: Hay House, 1984.

Jung, Carl. *Psychology and Alchemy*. New York: Pantheon Books, 1953.

Leadbeater, Charles. *Clairvoyance*. Seattle: Kessinger Publishing, 2012.

Yogananda, Paramahansa. *Autobiography of a Yogi*. Seattle: Self-Realization Fellowship, 2014.

To Write to the Author

If you wish to contact the author or would like more information about this book, please write to the author in care of Llewellyn Worldwide Ltd., and we will forward your request. Both the author and publisher appreciate hearing from you and learning of your enjoyment of this book and how it has helped you. Llewellyn Worldwide Ltd. cannot guarantee that every letter written to the author can be answered, but all will be forwarded. Please write to:

Kala Ambrose
℅ Llewellyn Worldwide
2143 Wooddale Drive
Woodbury, MN 55125-2989

Please enclose a self-addressed stamped envelope for reply, or $1.00 to cover costs. If outside the USA, enclose an international postal reply coupon.

Many of Llewellyn's authors have websites with additional information and resources. For more information, please visit our website at http://www.llewellyn.com.

GET MORE AT **LLEWELLYN.COM**

Visit us online to browse hundreds of our books and decks, plus sign up to receive our e-newsletters and exclusive online offers.

- **Free tarot readings • Spell-a-Day • Moon phases**
- **Recipes, spells, and tips • Blogs • Encyclopedia**
- **Author interviews, articles, and upcoming events**

GET SOCIAL WITH **LLEWELLYN**

 Find us on Facebook

www.Facebook.com/LlewellynBooks

Follow us on

www.Twitter.com/Llewellynbooks

GET BOOKS AT **LLEWELLYN**

LLEWELLYN ORDERING INFORMATION

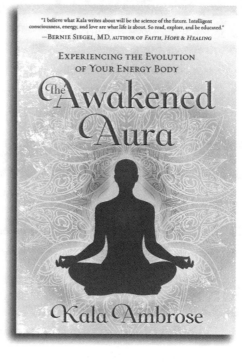

EXPERIENCING THE EVOLUTION
OF YOUR ENERGY BODY

The Awakened Aura

Kala Ambrose

The Awakened Aura
Experiencing the Evolution of Your Energy Body
KALA AMBROSE

Humanity is entering a new era—we are evolving into super-powered beings of light. Our auric and etheric bodies are experiencing a transformational shift as new crystalline structures form within and around our auras. Kala Ambrose, a powerful wisdom teacher, intuitive, and oracle, teaches how to connect with your rapidly changing energy body to expand your awareness and capabilities on the physical, mental, emotional, and spiritual levels.

This book contains a wealth of practical exercises, diagrams, and instructions. Learn how to interpret and work with the auras of others, sense energy in animals, and sense and balance the energy in buildings and natural locations. Discover how energy cords attach in relationships, how to access the akashic records through the auric layers, how to use elemental energy to enhance your auric field, and much more.

978-0-7387-2759-2, 240 pp., 6 x 9   **$14.95**
